# The Meaning of Things

## Applying Philosophy To Life

### A.C. Grayling

*'The meaning of things lies not in things themselves, but in our attitudes to them.'*

ANTOINE DE SAINT-EXUPÉRY

PHOENIX

A PHOENIX PAPERBACK

First published in Great Britain in 2001
by Weidenfeld & Nicolson
This paperback edition published in 2002
by Phoenix,
an imprint of Orion Books Ltd,
Orion House, 5 Upper St Martin's Lane,
London WC2H 9EA

Eleventh impression 2004

A CIP catalogue record for this book
is available from the British Library.

ISBN 0 75381 359 9

Printed and bound in Great Britain by
Clays Ltd, St Ives plc

'The pieces are neatly turned, well researched and dense with quotations and aphorisms from an impressive variety of writers and traditions. I admire the sheer courage displayed in such an undertaking . . . there is much to like'

Simon Blackburn, *Sunday Times*

'Their style is polished; their sentiments correct; their learning impeccable. Straight alpha material'

Edward Skidelsky, *Sunday Telegraph*

'There is no abstruse theory and no attempt to explain one philosopher's view of life in any detail. Grayling adopts a much lighter and more accessible approach. His pieces are admirably succinct, often no more than a couple of pages in length, but always he aims to open the reader's eyes to the subtleties inherent in concepts or values which have become so commonplace that we have committed the Socratic sin of ceasing to think about them . . . And, as the subtitle reveals, this is applied knowledge rather than mere theory, indicating a typically English view of philosophy: practical rather than metaphysical, thoughtful without being intellectual, and always deeply suspicious of grand theories and -isms (particularly postmodernism)'

Peter D. Smith, *Financial Times*

'Astute and informative'

Terry Eagleton, *Independent on Sunday*

'This enlightened and enlightening task . . . the whole thing is delightfully brainy'

*Private Eye*

'Here is an author who is certainly not cowed by large subjects . . . There is much fine, delicious writing here'

Noel Malcolm, *Sunday Telegraph*

'Dr Grayling combines wide learning with wise argument to fulfil the role he assigns to these essays – prompts to reflection'

Colin McCall, *Freethinker*

Dr A.C. Grayling is Reader in Philosophy at Birkbeck College, University of London, and is the author of numerous philosophical books. He is also a distinguished literary journalist and broadcaster, and his most recent book is the acclaimed biography of William Hazlitt, *The Quarrel of the Age*, published by Weidenfeld & Nicolson.

### By A.C. Grayling

The Refutation of Scepticism

Berkeley: The Central Arguments

The Long March to the Fourth of June
(as *Li Xiao Jun*)

Russell

China: A Literary Companion
(*with S. Whitfield*)

Moral Values

An Introduction to Philosophical Logic

Wittgenstein

Philosophy: A Guide Through the Subject

Philosophy: Further Through the Subject

The Quarrel of the Age:
The Life and Times of William Hazlitt

The Meaning of Things:
Applying Philosophy to Life

The Reason of Things:
Living with Philosophy

# Contents

Introduction vii

PART I
**Virtues and
Attributes**

Moralising 3
Tolerance 7
Mercy 10
Civility 12
Compromise 15
Fear 18
Courage 21
Defeat 24
Sorrow 26
Death 29
Hope 34
Perseverance 37
Prudence 40
Frankness 42
Lying 45
Perjury 48
Betrayal 51
Loyalty 54
Blame 56
Punishment 58
Delusion 60
Love 63
Happiness 71

PART II
**Foes and
Fallacies**

Nationalism 77
Racism 80
Speciesism 83
Hate 86
Revenge 89
Intemperance 92
Depression 96
Christianity 99
Sin 108
Repentance 112
Faith 116
Miracles 125
Prophecy 127
Virginity 130
Paganism 133
Blasphemy 136
Obscenity 138
Poverty 142
Capitalism 144

PART III
**Amenities and
Goods**

Reason 153
Education 157
Excellence 161
Ambition 163
Acting 165
Art 168
Health 170
Leisure 173
Peace 176
Reading 178
Memory 182
History 186
Leadership 189
Travel 192
Privacy 195
Family 198
Age 201
Gifts 203
Trifles 206

# Introduction

*Reader, lo! a well-meaning Booke.*
MONTAIGNE'S SALUTATION TO HIS READERS

In the preface to his little book of miscellaneous essays called *Guesses at Truth*, the nineteenth-century cleric Julius Hare wrote, 'I here present you with a few suggestions ... little more than glimmerings, I had almost said dreams, of thought ... If I am addressing one of that numerous class who read to be told what to think, let me advise you to meddle with this book no further. You wish to buy a house ready furnished; do not come to look for it in a stone quarry. But if you are building up your opinions for yourself, and only want to be provided with the materials, you may meet with many things in these pages to suit you.' There is little in common between Hare's outlook and the reflections which follow below, but with these words he provides a most suitable preface to them.

Socrates famously said that the unconsidered life is not worth living. He meant that a life lived without forethought or principle is a life so vulnerable to chance, and so dependent on the choices and actions of others, that it is of little real value to the person living it. He further meant that a life well lived is one which has goals, and integrity, which is chosen and directed by the one who lives it, to the fullest extent possible to a human agent caught in the webs of society and history.

As the phrase suggests, the 'considered life' is a life enriched by thinking about things that matter – values, aims, society, the characteristic vicissitudes of the human condition, desiderata both personal and public, the enemies of human flourishing, and the meanings of life. It is not necessary to arrive at polished theories on all these subjects, but it is necessary to give them at least a modicum of thought if one's life is to have some degree of shape and direction. To give thought to these matters is like inspecting a map before a journey. Looking at a map is not the same thing as travelling, but it at least provides orientation, a sense of place and of how places relate to each other – especially those one would like to visit. A person who does not think about life is like a stranger mapless in a foreign land; for one such, lost and without directions, any turning in the road is as good as any other, and if it takes him somewhere worthwhile it will have done so by the merest chance.

The discussions – the sketch maps – in the following pages are, with proper diffidence, put forward as prompts to reflection merely, or better: as contributions to a conversation. They are certainly not offered as definitive statements on the topics they address. And because I rarely live up to the virtues they extol, or avoid the vices they condemn, no claim to sainthood, still less sanctimony, is implied by them – far from it.

These discussions began as contributions to the *Guardian* newspaper, in the form of the 'Last Word' column in the Saturday Review, accompanied by Clifford Harper's brilliant illustrations. Most of them are short, some are longer. Each is self-contained, although neither their grouping nor their arrangement is arbitrary. Thus, comments on moralising are followed by some on tolerance, remarks on fear by some on courage, remarks on sorrow, death and hope are placed together, as are those on frankness and lying, betrayal and loyalty, blame and punishment. Other topics which naturally pair – love and hate, for example – can certainly be read together, but are placed apart for other reasons. Mainly, however, the discussions are meant to be read as separate self-standing pieces, and occasionally as clusters, but not as a sequence – for this is not a continuous treatise, but a miscellany prompted by commentary on the daily life of the human condition. They once each had the space of a week around them, adding to their self-containment. But just as all roads lead to Rome, so all these topics lead to one another by more and less direct routes, as a little reflection on the groupings shows.

The book is divided into three Parts, one of which concerns some of the things that are enemies to human flourishing, among them racism, nationalism, religion, revenge, poverty and depression. Doubtless, some will take offence at the inclusion of religion in this category. If all espousers of religion behaved like Quakers or shared the views of Theravada Buddhists, there would be little to quarrel with in religion save its super-naturalistic beliefs. But religion has for the greatest part been, and still remains, an affliction in human affairs, and cannot be omitted from discussion of the considered life.

Yet I believe passionately in the value of all things spiritual – by which I mean things of the human spirit, with its capacity for love and enjoyment, creativity and kindness, hope and courage. Although mankind is the author of much monstrous cruelty, of despoliation, greed, conflict and ugliness, it is also the author of much that is best in the world, which is a reason both for celebration and optimism. Some people seem unable to allow that mankind is the source of what makes the world bearable – pity, beauty and tenderness – nor that it is human genius which is responsible for the achievements of art and science. Such people have to believe in the existence of supernatural agencies as the source of the world's good, while fathering its evil exclu-sively on human beings. That is a calumny on mankind, as well as an irrational hangover from mankind's ignorant and fearful infancy, when nature was believed to be governed by invisible

# PART I
## Virtues and Attributes

# Moralising

*A man who moralises is usually a hypocrite.*

OSCAR WILDE

A moraliser is a person who seeks to impose upon others his view of how they should live and behave. Everyone is entitled to a view about what counts as acceptable behaviour, and everyone is entitled to put it forward as eloquently and forcefully as he can. But moralisers go much further. They want others to conform to their views, and they seek to bring this about by coercion – employing means which range from social disapproval to legal control, this latter often being their preferred option. In forcing others to comply with their preferences they show at least several of the following: insensitivity, intolerance, unkindness, lack of imagination, failure of sympathy, absence of understanding, ignorance of alternative interests and needs in human experience, and arrogance in believing that theirs is the only acceptable way. They defend their actions by saying that they are trying to defend others from harm, thereby claiming not only a monopoly on moral judgment, but the right to decide on others' behalf what is good for them.

When moralisers attack liberal legislation on homosexuality, abortion, prostitution, censorship, blasphemy, bastardy, and other like matters, it is their way of manifesting hostility to lifestyles they personally dislike, and of trying to impose instead their own choices, usually in the form of a traditionalist fantasy of 'family morality'. They claim to represent majority public opinion – an unreliable beast which few of them would wish to represent on other questions – but that is a dishonest manoeuvre. Their true motives are that they are afraid of attitudes and practices more relaxed than they can allow themselves to be – their timidity, their religious anxieties, their fear that they might themselves be, say, homosexual or libidinous, and a host of personal motives besides, drive them to stop the rest of the world thinking, seeing, or doing what they are afraid to think, see or do themselves.

When the body politic is immune to moralisers they merely appear comical – as prigs and curmudgeons who complain and blame, stamping their feet and waving umbrellas in outrage at whatever is different from themselves or comes too close to their own guilty desires. When the body politic is not immune to them they are a menace, causing not just general inflammation and irritation in society, but downright misery to the people whose ways of life differ from their own.

Every age thinks it is in crisis. Things have got worse, people say, clucking their tongues; crime is up, the quality of life down, the world in a mess. People of religious bent are inclined to think that their personal epoch is so bad that it probably marks the end of the world.

Such sentiments are misleading because they premise a belief that somewhere or sometime the world had something which has since been lost – a cosy, chintzy, afternoon-teatime era when there was neither danger without nor unease within. But when we begin rummaging among these myths to provide solutions to present-day troubles, which is what moralisers do, we are in trouble indeed.

Consider those who praise so-called 'Victorian values' and claim that if only we could return to them we would overcome the problems of our allegedly demoralised society. They tell us that we must do as the Victorians did by embracing family life, cleanliness, and godliness, and by working hard and being orderly. In their view Victorian virtue is exemplified by Mrs Nubbles, Dickens's widowed washerwoman who provided sustenance for her three children in a home that was extremely poor but had, in Dickens's words, an 'air of comfort about it' that comes with 'cleanliness and order'. It is symbolised by the Cratchits gathering for their poignantly limited Christmas 'feast'. It is summed up by the Victorian philanthropists who built libraries and schools. Let us learn the lessons here illustrated, the admirers of Victorian values say, and all will be well.

Their game is given away by their measures of society's 'demoralisation'. An often-chosen measure is the rising rate of what one of them (the historian Gertrude Himmelfarb) still refers to as 'illegitimate births'. This is evidence of a thoroughly Victorian and therefore question-begging view of vice. The very notion of 'illegitimacy' is so anachronistic that one wonders whether neo-Victorians understand the problems that modern society faces. Even the Church of England no longer speaks in such terms. For there is nothing remotely wrong with children being born to unmarried parents; but there is everything wrong with children being brought up in poverty. All the marrying in the world did not stop millions of Victorian children being physically and educationally stunted because of the inequities and inequalities of Victorian society, where poverty was grinding, the streets of London were vastly more dangerous than they are today, and market forces made child prostitution one of the capital's largest employers of child labour.

Those of us whose position on the food-chain is a comfortable one very much like the idea of those lower down the food-chain behaving themselves, being quiet and dutiful and clean, living well-ordered, sober, self-sufficient and self-helping lives, keeping their children in order and shackling themselves to the

# Tolerance

*The peak of tolerance is most readily achieved by those who are not burdened with convictions.*

ALEXANDER CHASE

Tolerance is a rare and important virtue. It has its limits, but they are usually drawn too tightly and in the wrong places. Consider the decision by a judge in Madrid who refused an application by the city's police to order prostitutes in the Casa de Campo to put on more clothes. The prostitutes there are scantily clad in suspenders, basques and the briefest of mini-skirts, which the police chief claimed is indecent; but the judge ruled that as that was the uniform of their profession, they were entitled to wear it.

Here was a Daniel come to judgment indeed. The ruling is tolerance itself, and would have been applauded by history's greatest prophet of this virtue, John Stuart Mill. In his seminal book *On Liberty* he wrote, 'Mankind are greater gainers by suffering each other to live as seems good to themselves, than by compelling each to live as seems good to the rest.'

This remark carries a number of significant implications. It defines an intolerant person as one who wishes others to live as he thinks they ought, and who seeks to impose his practices and beliefs upon them. It says that the human community benefits by permitting a variety of lifestyles to flourish, because they represent experiments from which much might be learned about how to deal with the human condition. And it iterates the premise that no one has the right to tell another how to be or to act, provided that such being and acting does no harm to others. These are the tenets of liberalism, a word of malediction among those who fear that unless a tight grip is kept on human thoughts and instincts, earth will break open and demons will rise.

Tolerance is, however, not only the centrepiece but the paradox of liberalism. For liberalism enjoins tolerance of opposing viewpoints, and allows them to have their say, leaving it to the democracy of ideas to decide which shall prevail. The result is too often the death of toleration itself, because those who live by hard principles and uncompromising views in political, moral and religious respects always, if given half a chance, silence liberals because liberalism, by its nature, threatens the hegemony they wish to impose.

To the question, 'Should the tolerant tolerate the intolerant?' the answer should therefore be a resounding 'No.' Tolerance has to protect itself. It can easily do so by saying that anyone can put a point of view, but no one can force another to accept it. The only coercion should be that of argument, the only obligation should be to honest reasoning. Helen Keller said that 'the highest result of education is tolerance', and she was right; one can be confident that in most cases the unbiased reasonings of an informed mind will come out in favour of what is good and true.

Intolerance is a psychologically interesting phenomenon because it is symptomatic of insecurity and fear. Zealots who would, if they could, persecute you into conforming with their way of thinking, might claim to be trying to save your soul despite yourself; but they are really doing it because they feel threatened. The Taleban of Afghanistan force women to wear veils, to stay at home, and to give up education and work, because they are afraid of women's freedom. The old become intolerant of the young when alarmed by youth's insouciance towards what they have long known and held dear. Fear begets intolerance, and intolerance begets fear: the cycle is a vicious one.

But tolerance and its opposite are not only or even invariably forms of acceptance and rejection respectively. One can tolerate a belief or a practice without accepting it oneself. What underlies tolerance is the recognition that there is plenty of room in the world for alternatives to coexist, and that if one is offended by what others do, it is because one has let it get under one's skin. We tolerate others best when we know how to tolerate ourselves: learning how to do so is one aim of the civilised life.

# Mercy

*He that spares the bad injures the good.*

THOMAS FULLER

In a letter to the Emperor Nero on the subject of mercy, Seneca wrote, 'So that we may not be misled by the plausible name of mercy into doing an opposite wrong, let us enquire what mercy is.'

Mercy is often a beautiful virtue, but occasionally a dangerous one. It is not pity, or kindness, or humanity; it is a specific form of restraint, by which one remits a punishment that is both deserved and due. It is a stopping short of the full penalty merited by wrongdoing. Mercy is often indeed prompted by kindness, or by pity or sympathy, but it is not the same thing as they. Often, when appeals are made on behalf of those who, say, are going to be shot for fraud (as in China) or stoned to death for adultery (as in Saudi Arabia), the appeal is not for mercy but for justice, because these activities do not merit such harsh punishment in the first place. In the strictest sense, therefore, the word 'mercy' relates only and specifically to withholding a properly deserved punishment. When we say that Gengis Khan butchered his foes 'mercilessly' we are using the term loosely, for we mean that he treated them cruelly or inhumanely. This looser use is now the commonest one.

The opposite of mercy is not strictness – which is a virtue

too; as Seneca says, 'one virtue cannot be the opposite of another' – but cruelty. To punish a malefactor more severely than he deserves is cruel. 'Let the punishment fit the crime' sang the Lord High Executioner; this is the meaning of 'condign' in 'condign punishment'.

Mercy is sometimes described as the support of justice. That is true when laws are unreasonable and unfair, because harsh laws create lawlessness, to prevent which a wise governor will use the opportunity of their harshness to show his own virtue of clemency. But the danger of mercy, even in these circumstances, is that it leads to its own undoing. Shakespeare might have given Portia words no less true than sweet to mitigate Shylock's legal due; but he has Timon tell a yet harder truth when he says, 'Nothing emboldens sin so much as mercy.'

There seems to be a consensus on that point. 'Pardon one offence,' says Publilius Syrus, 'and you encourage the commission of many.' Seneca himself, when not praising Nero for his reluctance to sign death warrants ('Oh that I knew not how to write!' repined the tyrant as he did so; Seneca had a good line in irony), has a character in his *Trojan Women* say, 'He who forbids not sin commands it.'

The chief reason for being merciful is that we all need mercy ourselves. It is a proper outcome of the pity our fellows prompt in us through our shared humanity; 'To understand all is to forgive all,' the French say. And as a general rule, what could be kinder or more civilised than to remit the moral debts that others incur, in the interests of a kinder world? But there is a limit. Those who showed no pity – those who tortured, murdered, beat, gassed, shot, raped, and repressed – and those who ordered them to do it, stepped beyond that limit. The long roll-call of such people in recent world history is too well known to need repeating here. Mercy is not merely wasted on them, it is a licence to others who think they might get away with it too. For them, mercy is misplaced: what is required is justice, for the world's sake.

# Civility

*The knowledge of courtesy is a very necessary study; like grace and beauty, it breeds mutual liking.*

MONTAIGNE

Despite appearances, the Western world is not undergoing a new immoral age. It is suffering a different phenomenon: a loss of civility, a deficit of good manners. What is often regarded as moral collapse is no such thing; western societies at the opening of the twenty-first century are by many measures better, in 'moral' respects, than a century ago: compare (say) Victorian London's sweatshops, hordes of child prostitutes, and violent street muggers. Rather, what has happened is a decay of what makes the social machine function – a breakdown of the mutual tolerance and respect that allows room in a complex plural society for individuals to live their own lives in peace.

Civility is a matter of mores, etiquette, politeness, of informal rituals that facilitate our interactions, and thereby give us ways to treat each other with consideration. It creates social and psychological space for people to live their own lives and make their own choices. Youths spitting on the pavement and swearing on buses offer merely superficial symptoms of incivility; more serious are such things as invasion of privacy by tabloid newspapers, and irruptions into areas of personal life irrelevant to public concerns – for example, exposés of the sex lives of politicians. Our age is in fact a moralistic one, nauseatingly so;

which is a large part of the problem – for moralistic attitudes are intolerant, and intolerance is one of the worst discourtesies. To ask for courtesy is, in one way, to ask for very little; 'We must be as courteous to a man,' Emerson remarked, 'as we are to a picture, which we are willing to give the advantage of a good light.'

The loss of civility means that social feeling has been replaced by defensiveness, with groups circling their wagons around 'identity' concepts of nationality, ethnicity and religion, protecting themselves by putting up barriers against others. Society fragments into subgroups whose members hope thereby to shield themselves against the abrasive selfishness and disregard of others.

'There is a courtesy of the heart,' said Goethe, 'which is akin to love. Out of it arises the purest courtesy in outward behaviour.' This states an ideal; it ignores the fact that civility can, of course, be a mask – it has always been open to abuse, and if we relearned our manners it would continue so; but that does not alter the main point, which is that civility fosters a society that behaves well towards itself, whose members respect the intrinsic value of the individual and the rights of people different from themselves.

Ill-mannered people are generally so because they falsely estimate their own worth, and think that a waiter (who is probably a medical student earning extra pocket money) or a bus driver (who is probably writing the next prize-winning novel in his spare time) is to be valued by his occupation – or more accurately, by his income, which in these cases could be assumed to be modest – rather than his humanity. There begins impertinence: make a person a label, or a sum of money, and he becomes not an end in himself, but an instrument; and to treat anyone as such is, as Kant argued, not just the supreme discourtesy but the supreme wrong.

'Civility is to human nature what warmth is to wax,' said

Schopenhauer. Although conflict is endemic to the human condition, it remains worthwhile to urge the claims of civility as a means at least of managing it. Even if one grants (as one should not) the relativist view that certain values are mutually irreconcilable, and even if there will never be a clear answer to how certain dilemmas should be resolved, still we can say that civility is our best hope for finding and maintaining that subtle and constantly renegotiated equilibrium on which the existence of society depends.

parties away believing that they have achieved this outcome by their own cleverness.

Whether compromise is appropriate in a given circumstance is entirely a matter of what is at stake. Between nations and states accommodation is rarely impossible, and it is almost always better than tariff war or shooting war. But the liberal democracies were right not to compromise with Hitler, and it is a tragedy that they now too often compromise with tyrants morally indistinguishable from Hitler. In many cases it is not difficult to decide whether to compromise, and the truth is that Western governments too often compromise with regimes guilty of human rights violations, aggression, and general delinquency, always with the aim of saving money and trouble at home, no matter how much cost in human agony is exacted abroad. And when difficult cases come, it is the mark of a mature political comity that it makes no compromises over the task of judging, nor over acting with resolve if required.

In private life – for a prime example: in domestic relationships – compromise is both a saviour and the destroyer. Obviously enough, no one can sustain a relationship without accommodating the other's character and some at least of his or her needs and ways. It means negotiation, always in the hope of constructive and mutually satisfactory adjustment. But the truism that people change over time is so often forgotten in relationships that failure, if it happens, comes as a surprise to the parties, who have missed their opportunities to renegotiate the old contract when new compromises were needed.

At the same time, too many relationships are premised on large compromises made by just one party to them. Traditionally it was women who made them, giving up whole-life possibilities to care for husbands, children, or elderly parents. Often the compromise concerns disparities in sexual interest, one party having to suffocate needs because the other fails to satisfy them – or to express them in such socially disapproved ways as adultery or resort to prostitutes, each itself a compromise that history and society have together reached as a way of containing the volcanic power of sex.

Most insidious of all is the compromise an individual makes with himself when ambitions start to falter, and he begins to 'accept his limitations' – a phrase that far more often denotes retreat and weariness in the face of failure than a just discernment of powers. Unamuno said that we are all potentially heroes and geniuses, if only we would have the courage, and do the hard work, necessary to becoming so. Perhaps – here finding the exception to Burke's rule – the one compromise we should never make is with life.

# Fear

*If the diver always thought of the shark, he would never lay hands on the pearl.*

SA'DI

It can be left to others to explain the psychology of recreational fear – the reason why many people relish horror films and hair-raising fun-fair rides – although one suspects it has fundamentally to do with the fact that the human central nervous system craves stimulation, which it can get either from within by the provocation of adrenaline and other endogenous substances, or from without in bottle, pill or ampoule form. These internal and external stimuli are rather like the salt and pepper some folk sprinkle on food; having lost sensitivity to delicate naturally occurring savours, they need condiments to provoke their taste-buds. So it is with other stimuli: the lover's touch, the hinted melody, the fascination of ideas, to some seem too pale a source of stimulation; for them the vindaloo of a horror film is the remedy. And why not? There is no disputing tastes.

But recreational fear is not true fear; and true fear is an enemy of endeavour. Fear, said Aeschylus, makes us weak. It subverts confidence, interferes with performance, lames resolve. And it distorts perceptions, creating obstacles and monsters where none exist: 'Fear is sharp-sighted,' said Cervantes, 'it sees things underground, and much more in the skies.' There is of course the thought that fear has a positive side; a capacity for fearing gives an obvious evolutionary advantage because it makes us alert to dangers. Moreover, as it has more than once been sagely remarked that a good scare is worth more to a man than good advice. But it remains that fear itself is more to be feared than most of the things people usually fear, and that gives pause for thought.

In addition to paralysing effective action, fear is the source of many social ills. It gives rise to superstitions and religions, to feelings of racial and tribal antipathies, to hostility to the new or different, to rigidity and conservatism, to adherence to outworn practices and beliefs whose only recommendation is their familiarity. The useful timidity that protects animals living insecurely in a hostile environment where predators roam, has thus become in modern mankind a liability. 'Fear can never make virtue,' said Voltaire. Ignorance and fear are closely allied; they feed from each other, and their appetite grows by feeding. And fear has its own inexorable logic: what we fear comes to pass far more rapidly than what we hope – mainly because we make it so.

Fear of death is one of the commonest fears, and one of the chief sources of cowardice. As the saying has it, the coward dies a thousand deaths, the courageous man only one. The same applies to fear of pain – the dentist's drill is suffered for hours in anticipation before the ten minutes of actuality. How is one to combat such fear? In the case of death the answer is to distinguish between death, as a state, and dying, as an activity. Some religious conceptions of an afterlife make the state of death a terrifying prospect – but most views of death are not so cruel, the kindest being the most rational, which is that death is a state of non-being, equivalent to the state of not yet being born. There is nothing to fear in that. Dying, which is an act of living, might be easy or difficult; only the latter invites anxiety; but it is consoled by the saying engraved on King David's ring, put there to make him thoughtful both when happy and when sad: 'This too will pass.'

Fears exist to be borne. No man is brave unless he is afraid. The saying of Sa'di about the shark and the pearl embodies all the wisdom required to combat fear; living just once, we have to attempt the pearl, or live with regret. And if there is anything worth fearing in the world, it is living in such a way that one gives oneself cause for regret in the end.

# Courage

*Courage is a kind of salvation.*

PLATO

Euripides said, 'A coward turns away but a brave man's choice is danger.' What the ancient Greeks learned, as the first truly intellectual and philosophical people, is that there is more danger to one's hopes, one's mettle, one's pride, in venturing into the battle of ideas, than in murdering a man who disagrees with you – and that doing so therefore takes proportionally more courage.

Most people tend to think of courage as a warrior virtue, as belonging typically to battle; and therefore, by analogy, to endeavour on the upper slopes of Everest, in the deeps of the sea, and even on the sports field – in other words, wherever endurance, grit and determination in the face of physical challenges are required. That is true enough. But courage is often demonstrated, because it is often needed, in greater quantities in daily life; and there are even times when 'merely to live', as Seneca put it in a letter to Lucilius, 'is itself an act of courage'.

Ordinary life evokes more extraordinary courage than combat or adventure because both the chances and inevitabilities of life – grief, illness, disappointment, pain, struggle, poverty, loss, terror, heartache: all of them common features of the human condition, and all of them experienced by hundreds of thousands of people every day – demand kinds of endurance and bravery that make clambering up Everest seem an easier alternative. Whereas mountaineering and deep-sea diving are self-contained activities that last a certain length of time with – if all goes well – a return to a *status quo ante* when they are over, facing (say) grief or disappointment is quite different. They are open-ended, new, different dispensations with unforseeables deeply embedded in them, promising only that much will have to be borne before relief comes. To lie sleepless with pain at night, or to wake every morning and feel the return of grief, yet to get up and carry on as best one can, is courage itself.

Moreover, courage can only be felt by those who are afraid. If a man is truly fearless as he leaps over the enemy parapet or hurls himself into a rugby tackle, he is not courageous. Because most people fail to recognise this simple fact, the true quantum of heroism in the world goes unrecognised and therefore unrewarded. The quaking public speaker, the trembling amateur actor, the nervous hospital patient submitting himself to needles and scalpels, are all manifesting courage. 'This is courage in a man,' Euripides further said, 'to bear what heaven sends.' Actually he said 'to bear unflinchingly', but by this addition he spoils the sentiment, because if courage requires fear, then flinching is perfectly in order.

Although ordinary life demands courage, sometimes in exceptional amounts, there is yet another kind of courage required for the task of being human: the courage to meet the new and to accept the different in the chances of experience. Rilke gave luminous expression to this idea in his *Letters to a Young Poet*, by saying that we need 'courage for the most strange, the most singular and the most inexplicable that we may encounter'. He meant the courage to accept love when it offers, to face death when it comes, to bear the burdens that life imposes in return for its gifts; and above all the courage to create something to mark our own individual responses to the world, however modest; for even when the courage to do this is unostentatious and private, it can make a crucial difference to the content or the quality of our lives.

# Defeat

*There are defeats more triumphant than victories.*

MONTAIGNE

At first blush it might seem that defeat and victory are the reverse and obverse of the same coin, each needing the other for either to have meaning. But although this is often so, it is not always so. There are defeats without corresponding victories, and vice versa, and there are defeats which are victories, and vice versa, and it is important to distinguish them – for otherwise one is at risk of seeing one's life as having too high a proportion of defeats to victories, which is very rarely true.

When stags fight each other at the commencement of the rutting season, those that lose experience a large drop in testosterone levels, while the victor's levels surge. The symmetry ensures that the victor's harem will be his alone. Whether or not human psychology is similarly a function of endocrine glands, it is certainly true that teams or troops who perceive themselves as defeated suffer an according collapse of will. Antoine de Saint-Exupéry exactly catches their mood: 'Defeat is a thing of weariness, of incoherence, of boredom,' he wrote, 'and above all, of futility.'

Almost any moment of defeat might feel as Saint-Exupéry describes, except when defeat is glorious. 'I would prefer to fail with honour,' says a character in Sophocles, 'than win by cheating.' Any number of reflective souls have seen that the deepest disappointments come from near-victories; to endeavour, but just to miss, is harder to bear than to realise one had better not endeavour at all. But the moment you recognise you were after all a contender, you understand that there are many sorts of victories, the most educative of them being these self-same near-misses. It is what we aspire to be that colours our characters – and it is our trying, not just our succeeding, which ennobles them.

In another of his plays Sophocles has a character remark that when you yield to friends, you win the victory. The idea of good defeats – those in which you learn, or give, or allow the better to flourish – is an important one. Spinoza wrote that weapons never conquer minds, only magnanimity and love; to be conquered by these things is a great victory in itself, because it is a response to what is best. To recognise an argument as sound, and to defer to it, or to grasp the justice of another's cause and to make way for it, are likewise victorious defeats.

Defeat is always an opportunity, even when, as far too often happens, what is genuinely the better cause has been crushed by the worse. In such cases one's sense of failure is very hard to bear, as is defeat by circumstances involving the natural injustice of the universe, which deprives one of wonderful opportunities by some irreversible stroke that had nothing or little to do with one's own efforts – such as illness or loss, war or economic disaster. But nothing happens without a lesson to offer, or without opening other routes into the future. Neither might be easy to see at the time, which is where patience plays its part. T. H. Huxley liked to tell the medical students under his guidance that 'there is the greatest practical benefit in having a few failures' (and this in a profession which, literally, buries its mistakes); and he is right. It takes only courage, or good sense, to see that the best lessons are usually the hardest; and defeat often counts among these latter. And that, in turn, prompts the thought that the only true defeat lies in letting defeat win.

# Sorrow

*Sorrow makes us all children again.*

EMERSON

When people die in an accident, suddenly and unexpectedly, with a terrible arbitrariness that seems unjust and cruel beyond description, there seem to be very few consolations for those left behind. In such cases there is no preparation, as with someone long ill; no sense of the quiet inevitability of great age; there is no closure, no proper leave-taking. Too much is left unfinished and unsaid. Even when soldiers go to war, the possibility of their never returning gives a significance to the farewells on the day they left, and that fact brings comfort later. What intensifies the tragedy of sudden accidental death is that none of these helps is available.

But there are sources of consolation nevertheless. One is that the dead do not wish the living to linger in sorrow. Rather, they wish them to grasp the truth expressed in Giraudoux's lines reminding us that comfort and an eventual return to happiness are always promised in grief: 'Sadness flies on the wings of the morning; out of the heart of darkness comes the light.' To demonstrate this, consider the following. Think of those you care about; imagine them mourning when you die; and ask yourself how much sorrow you would wish them to bear. The answer would surely be: neither too much, nor for too long. You would wish them to come to terms with loss, and thereafter to remember the best of the past with joy; and you would wish them to continue life hopefully, which is the natural sentiment of the human condition. If that is what we wish for those we will leave behind us when we die, then that is what we must believe would be desired by those who have already died. In that way we do justice to a conception of what their best and kindest wishes for us would be, and thereby begin to restore the balance that is upset by this most poignant of life's sorrows.

Another consolation is to be found in the fact that sorrow is almost always shared. 'Grief wounds more deeply in solitude,' Seneca wrote, 'tears are less bitter when mingled with others' tears.' Even if sharing sorrow does not lessen it, after a time it becomes a help in the process of recovery.

For someone in the midst of sorrow hope seems far away. But ordinary human nature is full of surprisingly deep courage, not least of the kind that makes hope and a return to happiness possible. Sorrow is said to be one of the profoundest teachers of wisdom – 'Grief should be the instructor of the wise,' said Byron, for 'sorrow is knowledge' – and one thing it teaches is its own role in the texture of things. No personal history is free from sorrow; that is a fact intrinsic to the social nature of our kind. To be related to others, whether through family ties, or in love or friendship, is to invite the probability of loss, and therefore the likelihood of sorrow. Some find consolation in the thought of a transcendent order which requites sorrow by bringing together, in a final and permanent reconciliation, those who have mourned each other. Others find consolation in secular terms; the Stoic philosophers of antiquity were wisest in saying, as Epictetus did, that although sorrows come from without, our reception of them is to some degree under our own command, enough to make it possible for us first to bear and then to master them, acquiring from them more insight into the human condition, and more sympathy for others, than we had before that mastery was complete.

But it remains true that we never quite get over the sorrow caused by losing those most loved; we only learn to live with it, and to live despite it; which – and there is no paradox here – makes living a richer thing. That is sorrow's gift, though we never covet it.

# Death

*To die is different from what anyone supposed, and luckier.*

WHITMAN

If we base our understanding of death on evidence rather than fear or desire, we are bound to accept it as a twofold natural process: the cessation of bodily functions, including consciousness, followed by the body's dispersion into its physical elements. Cessation of function and the beginning of physical transformation occur together at the moment of death; exactly what constitutes that moment is a matter of controversy, an important matter because many physiological functions can now be sustained artificially. But there is some agreement that brain death, because it irrevocably ends mental activity, marks the Rubicon.

In the rest of nature cessation of function, followed by transformation of the physical elements, is part of life's continuity. It is a commonplace, but an important one, that death and decay are the servants of life. Fallen leaves change into humus on which next year's seedlings feed: so the death and transformation of autumn is essential to spring. Death is therefore a condition of life and constitutes half its rhythm.

Human death does, however, differ crucially from the death of other things. Most humans have self-reflexive consciousness, and most self-reflexively conscious beings regard death as a loss of supreme possessions: awareness and agency. It is not that most humans, if they thought about it, would wish to live forever, at least in this world; Shaw's Methuselah suggests that endless existence would be intolerable. Rather, it is that death comes too soon for most of us, before our interest in the world, and in those we care about, is exhausted.

From the subjective perspective, being dead is indistinguishable from being unborn, or from dreamless sleep; and can therefore hold no terrors. What seems frightening is the prospect of dying. But dying is an act of living; it is something only the living do, and like most other such acts – eating, walking, feeling happy or ill – it might be pleasant or otherwise. But being dead is not something we experience. We experience death only in losing others, and the experience is one of grief. Accordingly, our own deaths are no part of our personal experience: each of us experiences only life, of which dying is part. In this sense, from the subjective perspective we are immortal.

Marcus Aurelius, the Roman emperor who was also a Stoic philosopher, said in his *Meditations* that when we die we lose only the present moment, for the past has ceased to be and the future has not yet come; so to comfort ourselves we have only to look around and ask, 'Is this present moment really worth keeping?' But Aurelius is wrong. We are each of us a compound of memories and hopes, and the present is where past and future meet in striving or exhaustion, triumph or despair: each of these states and many others are defined by the relationship of our past to our expectations. We are creatures of narrative; the next instalment of the story interests us crucially; therefore death, either of someone we love, or as the indefinite prospect of our own absence from the story, typically counts as evil.

To those who welcome death, by contrast, the present's mix of past and future has a special shape, distorted by anguish. There is a psychological point after which, for them, the next chapter has to be the last.

Most religions premise an afterlife. Some of them teach that it begins with a judgment bringing punishment or reward. Such notions are very useful for controlling the living. Some people find such notions psychologically supportive, others find that they make death more terrible – for them death becomes a strange country ruled by dangerous powers, into which we venture ill prepared. Sometimes the more devout a believer is, the more dreadful immortality can seem.

Plato said that in Utopia belief in a blissful afterlife should be encouraged so that the citizens, not fearing death, would be good soldiers. Many forms of religious fanaticism share this view. Even respectable religions can be militaristic; some even promise that death in battle grants direct entry to paradise. In such cases also, therefore, superstitions about death prove useful to priests and tyrants.

Because being dead is, on a naturalistic view, identical to being unborn, nothing about death itself makes it good or evil. It is only what it removes from us that makes it so. If it removes intolerable and interminable pain, it is good; if it removes opportunities, hopes, connections with the beloved, it is bad. Some argue that one's own death is never bad, because in death one cannot be aware of what is lost. It is the prospect of loss which is the evil, not the fact of it; so once again death is a problem only for the living. It is an avoidable problem, therefore, for one can ignore it. In the same way, one can avoid fear of dying by accepting and then ignoring its inevitability, so avoiding the coward's fate of dying in imagination a thousand times over. For these reasons Spinoza wrote that 'The meditation of the wise man is a meditation not on death, but on life.'

The fundamental question is how to deal with others' deaths. We grieve the loss of an element in what made our world meaningful. There is an unavoidable process of healing – of making whole – to be endured, marked in many societies by formal periods of mourning, between one and three years long. But the world is never again entire after bereavement. We do not get over losses; we merely learn to live with them.

There is a great consolation. Two facts – that the dead once lived; and that one loved them and mourned their loss – are inexpungeably part of the world's history. So the presence of those who lived can never be removed from time, which is to say that there is a kind of eternity after all.

How many of us, though, can succeed in feeling these truths as consolations? We are not good at coping with death, especially in our contemporary materialist age, with its pretence that we live indefinitely and that the fountain of happiness is purchasing power. Few face the fact of death squarely, or consider its nature clearly. For most, the premise is that death is evil; they avoid thinking about it, and even refuse to allow that anyone suffering exquisitely should be allowed its merciful embrace if he chooses.

We hide from death therefore, and we hide death from us, until the last moment: and especially until we have to face the deaths of others. Unless we are religious, with the kind of animal faith that Tolstoy's Levin admired in his serfs, the forms and formalisms of dealing with death are often too stiff and awkward to give real comfort. That might be different if we thought about death and its meanings more carefully, and provided ourselves with an unvarnished, uncompromising portrait of it as the greatest fact of life. Such a portrait would do well if it showed us that death is many things, few of them easy, but all of them conquerable if we have courage enough.

We find death far harder and stranger than our forefathers did. In earlier times death was ubiquitous, more present and familiar than most of life's pleasures. Its seat at every table, its dogging of every step and breath, made the world a different place. It certainly gave religion a fearful boost, as the only offer of security in a treacherous existence.

Nothing seems so dead as clematis in winter. But even as March winds batter one's garden, long green fingers open from the clematis's brittle twigs, seeking somewhere to take a grip on life. Commonplace observations of nature's declining and resurgent cycles must have been early sources of hope for mankind, faced with the pity and terror of death. As a result, resurrection stories abound in religion and myth, and it is no accident that Easter is a spring festival.

Such thoughts explain belief in life after death – and so does the fact of fear, and a yearning for justice. The point about fear is self-explanatory; the desire for ultimate justice is a dimmer aspiration for those who occupy snug niches high up the food-chain. We forget that, for the vast majority of people, now as throughout history, existence is a grim labour. The urbane voices that reach us from the past come from the few who had opportunities to speak or act; which was at the expense of armies of faceless, nameless strugglers with little to hope but that, in another dispensation of things, they might have a chance of a spell in the sun. Hopes for an afterlife are, in fact, a sad reflection on, and a condemnation of, the facts of this life. That should make us understand better Spinoza's dictum about the wise man, for it should help us see that if life for many makes them envy the dead, humanity has failed itself badly.

# Hope

*If it were not for hope, the heart would break.*

THOMAS FULLER

To people in parts of the world where ethnic and religious conflicts persist, often as a result of things that happened hundreds of years ago – an instance of mankind's tragedies past keeping their fatal grip on the future – the saying in Proverbs painfully applies: 'Hope deferred maketh the heart sick.' For such people, as for those seeking asylum in free, rich countries so that they can have the life denied them in their unfree and impoverished homelands, hope – for peace, for opportunity, for a new life – is their chief possession. It is hard to bear the thought of their disappointment when their hopes are denied.

It is taken for a truism that hope is essential to life. What would it be to have no hopes, to believe that things only get worse, to expect failure and anticipate defeat? That is scarcely conceivable. In good times, say those who approve of optimism, hope is a prompt to yet better things; in bad times it is a comfort, because it sustains the idea of relief or rescue, of reward or at least justice at last. Even at the very worst, when we accept that hopes deceive, we recognise that they nevertheless provide 'an agreeable route', as La Rochefoucauld put it, 'to the end of our lives'.

But there are always, of course, those who disagree. History, cynics say, shows that dark nights have often cost mankind less pain than false dawns. The deceitfulness of hope gives it a bad name; for every ten thousand men there are a million hopes, but very few are realised. It offers lies as truth, and traps people in vain pursuits, which lead them on to greater disillusionments later. 'Just as dumb creatures are snared by food, human beings would not be caught unless they had a nibble of hope,' Petronius remarked. Hope – so the cynics continue – is distorting; it makes what is genuinely ugly and bad in life appear no more than a temporary screen for what is beautiful and good. It is therefore allied to illusion: 'One day everything will be well, that is our hope,' said Voltaire; 'today everything is fine, that is our illusion.' The fact that hope always applies to the future makes it a cheaply purchased, endlessly renewable commodity – the latter because as old hopes die, new ones can be raised in their place as swiftly and easily as thought. But is a life of false hope, or mere hope, or nothing but hope, a finer and nobler thing than a life squarely based on facing realities, and knowing them for what they are? 'Hope is the worst of evils,' Nietzsche famously said, 'for it prolongs the torment of man.'

It might be argued that cynics start from the wrong premise. They observe the human propensity to day-dream and fantasise, to cling to vain hopes in the face of overwhelming contrary evidence, to nurture unrealistic expectations and ambitions. They fail to recognise that out of this compost sometimes grow surprising blossoms of novelty and success. Most of what has moved the world onwards began as a hope; all of what has moved it backwards has involved the death of hopes.

The tough view that interprets hope as a weakness rather than a virtue says that we must pull up our socks and embrace Truth. But the only indisputable truth about the human condition, say hope's defenders, is that we can suffer, and that we shall die. The rest is for us to create. What would we make of ourselves without hope? We could adopt the posture of nihilism:

but that is a life worse than death. For some, indeed, death is hope's only alternative. Albert Camus identified philosophy's central question as 'Shall I commit suicide?' for if the answer is 'No', the implication is that there are things worth hoping for. Cynics object to treating hope as a virtue because it rarely bears fruit. But that, say hope's defenders, is to see things upside down. Hope is a virtue independently of its realisations; it is an intrinsic value, an end in itself, allied to courage and imagination, a positive attitude full of possibility and aspiration. For that reason you discover more about a person when you learn about his hopes than when you count his achievements, for the best of what we are lies in what we hope to be.

# Perseverance

*Many strokes overthrow the tallest oaks.*

JOHN LYLY

Courage and hope both depend on a crucial virtue: perseverance, the ability to keep going in adverse circumstances – with a cheerful countenance if possible, but if not, then at least in the spirit of Seneca's world-weary observation, 'Even after a bad harvest there must be sowing.'

It is said that perseverance is a good trait except when applied to inappropriate aims. This places the emphasis on knowing when aims are the right ones. Someone might say that the tone-deaf, lump-fingered man who persists in his endeavours to master the violin is obviously on the wrong tack, and it does not help to praise him for persevering. But someone else might reply that any worthy aim, such as playing the violin, dignifies the struggle to achieve it, and however difficult it might be for such a man to learn to play, he has still gained much from trying.

This is an encouraging reply. Arguably, most of us could do most of what we desire – or at least, like the aspiring violinist, could gain a great deal from trying – if we found the right way to approach it. I mean things like learning Mandarin or the mandolin, or reducing one's weight or overdraft. Some techniques suit some people, others suit others; one has to find the method best adapted to oneself. Of course certain things, like getting into the crew of the Shuttle spacecraft or becoming President of the United States, are probably less worth aiming for unless the antecedent conditions are right – if you are a supremely fit jet pilot with a physics degree you might entertain faint hopes of at least one of these offices. But they are peculiar avocations, not part of the range of human aspirations and activities that are reasonable enough, even if hard enough, for most.

One of John F. Kennedy's speech-writers left a fingerprint on history in 1961 with the brilliant remark that America was going to put a man on the moon by the end of that decade not because it was an easy thing to do, but because it was a hard thing to do; and doing hard things is what makes you better. Anything that requires perseverance is a hard thing in the meaning of this saying, and therefore improves you. The secret to persevering is an understanding of the 'learning curve', a graph with a line that rises, then dips somewhat, only to rise higher – and so on, rising then dipping then rising again, continuously to the top of the page. It represents the standard shape of the progress people make in mastering anything new. All goes swimmingly; then suddenly one seems to regress, to lose what advance has been made. At this point most people give up. But if they were to persist they would find that each dip is followed by a higher rise, and the overall pattern is upward and onward, making true the Latin motto, *Per ardua ad astra*.

It is a commonplace that perseverance tends to be more successful than violence – dripping water wears the stone that could not be hammered to pieces. It suggests a number of further traits in anyone who perseveres: determination, ambition, strength of resolve. The cynic would say that we should frequently substitute 'obstinacy', 'folly' and 'blindness' respectively. The opposite of perseverance is giving up, trying something else, abandoning ambitions. Let it be conceded that if the ambition was to join the Shuttle crew, the decision was probably wise; but generally speaking the best and most satisfying choice is to see things through. As Ruskin said, it is not what we get but what we become by our endeavours that makes them worthwhile.

# Prudence

*He does well who moors his boat with two anchors.*

PUBLILIUS SYRUS

Without doubt, prudence is a virtue. As the Ashanti say, 'No one tests the depth of a river with both feet.' It is a rich concept, central to much ethical thinking about the life well lived. It has the same root as 'providence' – *prudentia* and *providentia* are Latin alternatives – but in English the meanings have diverged. In its non-theological sense, to be provident is to be well provided by one's own foresight and care in the necessities and amenities of life. It therefore relates to the material state of the prudent individual. Prudence is a matter of character; to be prudent is to be careful, cautious, shrewd; it means governing one's tongue, husbanding one's resources, avoiding dangers, maintaining a reserve, thinking ahead, preparing. The opposites of prudence – rashness, fecklessness, haste; and most of us are at times guilty of these in various degrees – make life infinitely harder to live.

To live with discretion and forethought is to live as Aristotle recommended, in describing the good life as one governed by reason. His ideal was the man of *phronesis* – 'practical wisdom' – who always seeks the Golden Mean in any circumstance: courage, for example, is the mean between cowardice and rashness, as generosity is the mean between miserliness and profligacy. Aristotlean man – like the wise little mouse of Plautus, which 'never entrusts its life to one hole only' – is prudence personified.

But the middle way of Aristotle is, his critics say, middle in all ways: middle-aged, middle-browed, conservative, morally and emotionally flat. 'So soon as prudence has begun to grow up in the brain, like a dismal fungus,' wrote Robert Louis Stevenson, 'it finds its first expression in a paralysis of generous acts.' This is tantamount to warning that prudence too often blocks the road to progress. The bold, adventurous, daring act, the quick response, the impulsive choice, even the taking of risks, are what have led to change and growth, both in personal lives and in mankind's fortunes. Prudence is a cold and plodding virtue beside such vivacities. It seems not to belong in the intellectual economy of those who, realising that we only live once, take their chances by both lapels, agreeing with Blake that 'Prudence is a rich, ugly old maid courted by Incapacity', and wanting no part of her.

But as often happens, there is only apparent conflict here. Impulse is not necessarily imprudence, nor does a normally thoughtful life exclude trust in the emotions and instincts. There is a larger prudence in living boldly, because more possibilities for love and knowledge open that way. And the adventurer who paddles up the Amazon in pursuit of excitement is more likely to find it, and to tell us about it later, if he remembers the advice of Publilius Syrus when he moors his canoe for the night.

# Frankness

Politicians soon learn that frankness is an expensive commodity in public life. The same is true in private life, except when it is judiciously employed and tempered by kindness; for frankness can do greater harm to others than to oneself.

To speak frankly is to reveal what one really thinks, to tell the truth exactly as one sees it, and to do so whatever the consequences. When people are not frank they are being careful, or dishonest, or tactful – and often enough all three. Many find that dishonesty and tact are far more useful for getting on in life than frankness. This is regrettably true as regards dishonesty, but not always so as regards tact; for tact is an expression of concern for others' needs and sensitivities, and is an important instrument in helping people negotiate the unpredictable complexities of relationships.

The only kind of person who can always be frank is the saint who has no tincture of spite or small-mindedness in his character. He says what he thinks, and even when it is uncomplimentary to his interlocutors they sense that there is no malice in him and therefore they take no offence. But there are few such people in the world, and since the rest of us cannot guarantee the purity of our motives in speaking bluntly to others, politeness acquires a great value. In every social transaction most of us are consciously or otherwise at work, assessing how much frankness the circumstances can bear. Occasions differ; someone in a hurt or vulnerable state might need a few kind indirections to survive his crisis; an assembly of dinner guests might be offended by inappropriately chosen or presented facts, or bored by too large a quantum of them – so in both cases tact is in order. Tact is an intelligent virtue; everyone can be frank, even (perhaps: best of all) the simple and careless; but not everyone can finely adjust how and what he says to ameliorate human intercourse, through which more good is likely to come than otherwise.

Frankness is often a weapon deployed to wound or take revenge. We might sometimes tell people home truths because we are concerned for their welfare, but more often because we are inspired by hurt, jealousy or anger. 'All cruel people describe themselves as paragons of frankness,' Tennessee Williams observed. And the point about 'home truths' is that they – and with them, frankness in general – do not invariably reflect the truth properly so called. Often it is only what one thinks or claims is the truth – or, even worse, one's own unvarnished opinion – which is offered by one's bluntness. Thus it has much more to do with belief than fact, and the former, as a more subjective commodity, is always more likely to be tendentious. Noting that it is easy to be outspoken when you do not pause to tell the whole truth adds an important consideration: that you will succeed in properly serving both the truth and your fellow man only if you tell the whole truth, which requires much more thought and preparation than mere plain speaking does.

There is one arena where frankness is almost invariably a good thing: in the evolution of friendship. The point at which friends can drop their reserve and reveal themselves to each other is the point at which their relationship advances to a higher level. 'One frankness invites a reciprocal frankness, and draws forth discoveries, like wine and love,' wrote Montaigne. Such are franknesses of the heart, which give another access to one's self, and oneself access to another's self: and without such mutualities life would be worth little.

# Lying

That lies should be necessary to life is part and parcel of the terrible and questionable character of existence.

NIETZSCHE

In the related arts of politics and government, judicious econ-omies with truth are a stock-in-trade; neither art would be possible without them. We accept the necessity at times for evasions, equivocations, dissemblings and downright false-hoods in the practices of public life, and regard as naive anyone who insists otherwise. At the same time it is universally agreed that lying is in itself wrong, and the discovery of a lie always impugns the liar – indeed, a single lie can destroy a whole reputation for integrity.

Plato said that lies are not only evil in themselves, but infect the soul of those who utter them. He thereby states the uncom-promising view that a moral life has room only for truth. And the point generalises to social life: 'In plain truth, lying is an accursed vice,' wrote Montaigne; 'we have no tie upon one another, other than the reliability of our word.' But these austere views are not universally shared. Lying finds champions in those who recognise that without lies people would have no inner privacy, that life might be infected with boredom and despair, and much evil could result.

We second Homer's applause for Odysseus's cunning and fam-ously foxy deceits – he was a liar consummate in word and deed, elevated to heroic stature, who could outwit sirens, the giant Polyphemus, the witch Circe, and assorted denizens of Hades. Yet we agree that society can only operate on an assumption of probity; for the ordinary transactions of daily life we have to believe that most people are telling the truth most of the time. In thus having a deeply divided attitude to lying – accepting its utility, even necessity, but maintaining a strong background disapproval of it as if to keep it somehow within limits – we imply that there are sometimes justifications for lying. And that means we disagree with Plato.

Some argue that lies are justified when truth would gratuitously cause or heighten conflict. Moreover, they say, lies can be merciful, in protecting people from agonising knowledge; as when a doctor tells a terrified patient that all is well. And we can think of countless cases where lies promote harmony, restore justice, remedy injustice, counteract worse lies, and protect important truths. In all these cases what justifies the lie is the benefit of its outcome; if more good than harm flows from its telling, it is justified.

What troubles those like Plato who find lying unacceptable no matter what the consequences, is this: to tell a lie you have to know the truth but deliberately intend to communicate its very opposite to your audience. (If you tell your audience something which is false but which you do not know is so, you are not lying.) You thus commit a double crime: of knowing but concealing truth, a precious possession; and of purposefully leading others away from it. The hard justice of this view led later philosophers, notably Kant, to box clever in the way only philosophers know how. Lying is always wholly unacceptable, he said, but it is all right sometimes to tell an untruth, which is a different and lesser thing; where lying outright is like poisoning someone, telling him an untruth is like attacking him in the street (these are Kant's own similes) – a more honest thing, so to say. It is accordingly acceptable to tell an untruth when it protects the other from injury, to his feelings or otherwise. 'Am I ugly?' asks your neighbour, who makes Quasimodo look like a beauty queen. 'I wouldn't use the word "ugly",' you reply; 'you have a distinctive face.' Even religious moralists agree; they say that the Bible cautiously licenses Kantian untruths, as when Proverbs say, 'When words are many, transgression is not lacking; but the prudent are restrained in speech', and the Kirk in Scotland teaches that it is a sin to tell an untimely truth.

So we accept, even sometimes applaud, 'white lies', and recognise that the truth need not always be the whole truth. In the end, though, one is left with the feeling that Nietzsche is right: the fact that lies are necessary says much that is uncomplimentary to life, for it means that human relationships are never truly free of the unease and tension which sensitivities, jealousies and uncertainties bring.

# Perjury

*Deceive not thy physician, confessor, or lawyer.*

GEORGE HERBERT

The perjury law in the State of Indiana says that it is not enough to be truthful when testifying in court, you have to be logical too; for you commit perjury not only if you make a statement under oath which, as the statute has it, you either know to be false or which you do not believe to be true – a nice distinction – but also if you make two or more statements which are inconsistent with each other to such an extent that at least one of them has to be false. Since almost all of us hold inconsistent beliefs, we would do well to say as little as possible if we find ourselves in an Indiana witness stand.

The actual wording of Indiana's perjury statute is that statements have to be 'inconsistent to the degree that one of them is necessarily false', which in enjoining logic on the populace by law, is itself illogical – not in the sense that it is illogical to wish people to be logical, however hopeless an ambition that may be, but rather in the sense that the statute itself, on a literal reading, is illogical. And even on a generous reading it requires far too much.

The problem is loose wording, a fault that drafters of legal instruments are usually keen to avoid. The statute should require that statements are inconsistent to the degree that they cannot be true together, but it cannot require that whichever of them is false should be a 'necessary falsehood'. In the strict technical sense of logic, a statement is necessarily false when it cannot possibly be true – when, in short, it is self-contradictory. But both members of an inconsistent pair of statements can be self-consistent, in the sense that their respective truth and falsity could have been the other way round if the world had been different. This is what distinguishes a commonplace falsehood from a 'necessary' one; the latter cannot be true under any circumstances. The mere fact that one statement is inconsistent with another is no guarantee that either of them is necessarily false in this sense. And it is too lenient on perjurers to indict them for contradictions only.

Nevertheless, the intention of the Indiana statute is clear, and it captures the aim of perjury laws everywhere. Perjury is a serious crime because it directly undermines the purpose of proceedings at law, which is to try to do justice. Justice cannot be done unless the parties to a case provide the court with statements they sincerely believe to be true, and which convey all the relevant information in their possession. Since the very possibility of justice depends on this, all jurisdictions are severe in their punishment of perjury when they detect it.

Naturally enough perjury is committed all the time, usually because someone wishes to save his skin, but occasionally in hopes of serving a greater good. But even the latter is rarely a good excuse for it. The reason that lying in court is called perjury rather than simply lying, is that it is lying on oath. A party to a court case swears to the court, either on the Bible or by affirmation, to tell the truth. Taking an oath is no light matter; it is an undertaking to play a responsible part in the serious business of getting justice done. Membership of society carries with it a tacit commitment to play a responsible part in general, but the deliberate and public avowal of that pledge in court is a special act, and perjury is the perversion of it.

Optimistically, the law assumes that there is such a thing as truth, and that any individual can tell all of it, not only with no trace of falsehood tainting it, but without any admixture of mere probability or surmise. But the delicate question of whether truth exists, or is attainable, is in this sphere not the point. The absolute language of the oath has a pragmatic purpose: which is to enjoin witnesses to strive not to mislead the court, because if they succeed in doing so they murder justice.

This is why it does not matter whether the subject of a perjury is trivial or crucial. The mere fact of perjury is, by itself, matter crucial enough; for justice is one of the highest yet one of the most fragile of values, and its enemies cannot be given quarter.

# Betrayal

*All a man can betray is his conscience.*

JOSEPH CONRAD

There can be no betrayal if there is no pre-existing trust. When someone is accused of betraying country or friends or spouse, the accusation carries large assumptions about what an individual's obligations are in each case – obligations which tell us much about what is intrinsic to being a citizen, a friend, or a lover.

The trust which is broken when betrayal occurs is often unspoken. The belief that one has a special obligation to one's country, a loyalty dignified in the word 'patriotism', carries with it a raft of hidden suppositions: that one's country trusts one to defend it against aggression, whether by foreigners without or traitors within; that one will serve its interests, defend its honour, uphold its traditions, and merit its praise thereby. 'What a pity it is,' lamented Addison, 'that we can die but once for our country!' Early Roman history is full of patriots like Horatio and Mucius Scaevola, who shared Addison's view; they had before them, as a warning and a reproof, the example of the legendary betrayer Antenor, whose treachery delivered Troy to the Greeks.

Oddly, patriotism is most virulent in countries which do least for their citizens in the provision of welfare – the United States and China, for instance. The explanation is inferable from the sentiments displayed when a national football team is in action: there is something tribal, or territorial, about patriotism, and it is intimately connected with the citizen's sense of identity, in such a way that he feels pride in having a share of the nation's victories, even if that means having a share in its humiliations too. Any derogation from the sentiments of patriotism is construed by lovers of the 'fatherland' as a form of betrayal; but worst is the kind that delivers the country's secrets or security into hostile hands. In the past this put at risk the personal tenure of power of a monarch, which is why the punishments for treason were so severe. And although it is illogical to think so, the more savage the punishment, the worse we take the crime to be.

Betrayal of a person is far worse than betrayal of a country. To a reflective mind the latter is anyway an odd notion; a 'country' or 'nation' is an abstraction, almost invariably the product of war or dispossession of someone else – which is why some alleged betrayers have rebutted the charge by saying that to betray one must first belong: and one might never feel a sense of belonging. E. M. Forster said that if he was forced to choose between betraying his country or his friends, 'I hope I would have the guts to betray my country.' That implies what most would accept, that the trust implicit in the bond of friendship is deeper and more significant than almost any other. Friendship – in Aristotle's view the supreme human relationship – is many things, but at its core is the expectation that it will not merely survive injuries done or suffered, but will be supportive through them. 'The proper office of a friend is to side with you when you are in the wrong,' Mark Twain said. In the normal course of events betraying a friend takes such forms as passing on his confidences as gossip; in the extreme, it takes the form of giving his name to the secret police. It was the latter that Forster had in mind, but the former is betrayal enough.

Talk of betrayal also applies to lovers' infidelities. These are a constant theme in the narratives of Western culture, where there is a presumption of exclusivity in intimate relations, such that when one of a pair of lovers finds that the other is intimate with someone else also, he feels that his confidence has been violated and a promise – whether spoken or not – has been broken. The feeling of exclusivity is natural to the period of greatest infatuation, and its betrayal is truly such, because it means that the betraying party is only pretending that passion. But it is questionable whether the accidents of infatuation should be allowed to place one person's sexual and emotional expression into the exclusive lifelong possession of another. Fidelity should be freely given, not demanded as a right by the other party; and the concept of betrayal therefore does not apply when the gift is withheld or withdrawn.

# Loyalty

*A jewel in a ten-times-barr'd-up chest*
*Is a bold spirit in a loyal breast.*

SHAKESPEARE

Loyalty is a virtue, but only when it is principled. Unquestioning allegiance to a cause, a faith or an individual is bad because by its nature it is too easily made an instrument of wrongdoing – and indeed amplifies wrongdoing, for when instructions are blindly followed they are thereby potentiated. Even as an instrument of good its value is equivocal; a loyal servant is the mere vehicle of another's intentions, therefore little praise is due to him beyond the mere fact that he yields himself to his master.

The concepts most associated with loyalty are constancy, fidelity and trustworthiness. These can be virtues indeed, and the fact that they play a central role in loyalty explains why we think well of it. Generally, in praising loyalty we really mean to praise one or more of these virtues, and when we decry it – as when the Stalinist *apparatchik* carries out a purge, and the SS officer a gassing – we describe it as mistaken or blind. But if it can be these things, it only deserves its positive light when it represents a principled adherence to something independently defensible as good.

Loyalty to a verifiable good is not a requirement in politics, where, on the contrary, Elbert Hubbard's dictum that 'An ounce of loyalty is worth a pound of cleverness' very much applies. An individual politician is seen by his party as feet for the voting lobbies, and a mouth for the propaganda war. To be loyal in party terms means being quiescent, obedient and obliging. Loyalty to principle, to constituents, or to a cause which happens not to be party policy, is regarded as rank disloyalty. This is what offends independent minds on both right and left, thinking of their forerunners: the former, of the bluff squires of Walpole's day, stubbornly forming their own views no matter what the Crown's ministers wanted; the latter, of their roots running deeply via Dissent to Wat Tyler and beyond. It is a fact of history that independent-mindedness has more often been found in the latter camp than the former.

In personal life loyalty is a less equivocal virtue. In friendship it means standing by someone despite occasions of disagreement and disapproval, for friendship is first about fidelities and only afterwards about what tests them. The component virtues of constancy and trustworthiness are especially valuable in friendship when troubles come, because they are an infinitely greater comfort to anyone sleepless in the dark night of the soul than such impersonal helps as medications, counsellors or prayers.

'Men's minds are given to change in hate and friendship,' said Sophocles, which explains some of the rifts and reconciliations seen in public life. In public life, though, every blow of disloyalty against one who stands naked to the general gaze is, by that very fact, trebled in the harm it does, thus making disloyalty in statecraft a kind of assassination – sometimes needful, sometimes wanton.

# Blame

*Most of man's misfortunes are occasioned by man.*

PLINY THE ELDER

In circumstances of betrayal or tragedy the instinct to lay blame is overwhelmingly strong, because whether or not doing so is appropriate, it is almost the only relief for painful emotions. Sometimes the target of blame is obvious, sometimes not; but loss and grief must have their scapegoats.

Wherever particular blame, if any, is to be laid for the tragedies occasioned by wars and massacres, there is certainly a general blame. It lies on humankind for its propensity to make war and preparations for war, allowing such vast social resources to go into the production and operation of machineries of death – guns, bombs, landmines, hand-grenades, tanks, airplanes, sophisticated military engineering, millions of men, even more millions of tons of explosive steel, all round the world, specifically dedicated to the task of killing other humans and smashing the physical fabric of civilisation. If there were no war, no conflict, no jealousy between peoples, there would be no guns and bombs. That is where the blame lies: on us, because we all supinely accept – thinking that we are being sensibly realistic – that armies and weapons are inevitable. It lies on us because we accept, even if tacitly, that violence and its instruments are necessary features of the world. The acceptability of preparations to kill other people is the source of all the tragedies, great and small, that come from our arming the whole world with instruments of death, by which thousands therefore duly die, all round the world, every year.

Whereas blame is justified in this universal sense, it is by contrast inappropriate in an important aspect of the particular, namely, in the breakdown of personal relationships, where it likewise tends to be endemic. One way of recovering from these smaller tragedies is, in fact, to learn how to stop blaming. There is a futile symmetry in domestic blame: a man blames his wife for having an affair and leaving him, while she in turn blames him for what the lawyers call 'constructive desertion', perhaps (and usually) by failing to answer her need for intimacy and thereby driving her away. When we cease laying blame we either take responsibility for our own contributions, or become free to recognise that blame is irrelevant: for such things happen as part of the whirligig of life, and laying blame is a waste of energy which could be better directed at repairing damage or starting afresh.

# Punishment

*Crime and punishment grow out of one stem.*

EMERSON

Proverbs famously says, 'He that spareth his rod hateth his son'; which brings to mind the more sardonic Chinese saying, 'Beat your child every day; if you don't know what for, he certainly does.'

What is punishment for? There is a deep tension in our views about how to treat wrongdoing, whether in the minor form of infringements by a child testing the boundaries of permission in his small world, or the major form of such gross crimes as rape and murder. Do we punish to reform the wrongdoer, or to take revenge on him? Do we punish to deter others from doing wrong? Are such forms of punishment as execution and imprisonment ways of protecting society against malefactors, or means of exacting a repayment in kind – in suffering or durance – from them?

We cannot claim that imprisonment is all of these things at once; for if someone wished to wreak revenge, or to penalise, he might subject criminals to the treadmill or the cat-o'-nine tails, whereas if he wished to reform them, and return them to society as useful and self-sufficient citizens, he would treat them decently, and educate them in a profession or trade. Moreover, although it is right to think of protecting society from wrongdoers, we invite a problem if we push the thought too far. On severe principles such as 'three strikes and you're out', which takes criminals who will not or cannot rehabilitate and locks them away permanently, we bind ourselves to support, at the public charge, an enemy of society for the rest of his days. This gives fuel to proponents of capital punishment, who say we should simply rid ourselves of them. But that, in turn, is to stoop to the recourse of the worst criminals themselves.

Epictetus remarked that anywhere is a prison if you do not wish to be there. That suggests you can punish people effectively, at least for lesser crimes, by making them perform community service, or obliging them to observe a curfew, or to work extra hours to repay their victims. Both recompense and penalty are thereby combined.

According to some, any form of punishment is an evil; that is Jeremy Bentham's view. To punish someone is to deprive him of liberty or property, or even, in some jurisdictions, of life. These things are wrongs in themselves, and therefore need a special justification if society is going to do them. To justify punishment, society must first define crime; and there's the rub. In the past, for example, sumptuary laws made it a crime for anyone below the rank of earl to wear purple silk. You could be burned at the stake for rejecting church dogma. Until recently sex between consenting adult males was a crime. So, what counts as a crime changes, and with it what justifies punishment. It takes confidence to be sure, always, that we have our sense of crime and punishment right.

What of the question at the other end of the scale: it is of course needful to correct and even to punish a child for its own sake. But is it right sometimes to punish a child by, say, smacking? Here Rabindranath Tagore has the appropriate last word: 'He only may chastise,' he wrote, 'who loves.'

# Delusion

*Delusion is the child of ignorance.*

THE BHAGAVADGITA

In an incident not so long ago a 500-strong group of Mayan Indians in Guatemala attacked a party of Japanese tourists and killed two of them. The tourists had stopped to photograph children wearing local colourfully embroidered dresses. The Mayans thought that the photographs were destined to appear in a catalogue used by child kidnappers. Some reports described the Mayans as undergoing delusions to the effect that tourists steal children, and appealed to the phenomenon of the 'madness of crowds' to explain their lynch-mob behaviour.

Delusion is a vivid false belief, often felt by its victim to be threatening or exciting, and often associated with psychotic states. Normally sane people can suffer delusions when caught up in group hysteria, which explains crowd violence and mass witnessings of miracles. Demagogues like Hitler have always appreciated the advantage of bringing people together in large numbers, the better to influence and motivate them by non-rational means.

Delusion is not the same as illusion. In its primary meaning, illusion is a misleading sensory experience, whose sources are physical rather than psychological. Entertainers who perform 'magic tricks' are aptly called Illusionists. But the word can be applied to beliefs or hopes, as when we speak of someone's illusions about his wife or his job, and in this usage it means a systematic misapprehension – a weaker and less sinister state than delusion, making illusion the product of mistake rather than pathology.

Leaving aside cases in which it is produced by psychosis, and therefore is the result of disturbed brain chemistry, delusion is rightly said by the Bhagavadgita to have ignorance as its mother. Her other offspring include superstition, prejudice and folly. 'Ignorance is the womb of monsters,' Henry Ward Beecher said. There is a familiar tradition which elevates ignorance above knowledge, as a happier, more innocent state of being. The eighteenth-century cult of the 'noble savage' extolled the supposed freshness and serenity of a life unencumbered by knowledge, a life bounded only by the sky's visible horizon and the natural lifespan of man. 'Where ignorance is bliss,' Thomas Gray famously wrote in his lines on Eton College, 'it is folly to be wise.'

But that tradition is wrong. Ignorance is too fertile in wretchedness and tragedy, too ripe in error and falsehood, ever to stand comparison with knowledge. 'Ignorance is not bliss,' said Philip Wylie, 'it is oblivion.' It is the source of the great popular delusions of history – the Mississippi Scheme and the South Sea Bubble, absurd beliefs in alchemy, witchcraft, astrology, ghosts and (as new additions) alien abductions and UFOs. It is largely forgotten now that almost everyone in the sixteenth and seventeenth centuries in Europe believed that malevolent persons were busy poisoning food stores, water supplies, even the fish in the sea, using a colourless, odourless, undetectable substance called Aqua Tophana, which was said to do its fatal work with insensible slowness. An unpopular person had only to be labelled a poisoner to be lynched by a mob.

Was the Mayan attack a product of delusion? In remoter areas of Guatemala lynch justice is a common resort; and it is a fact that numbers of children – of all ages from infants to teenagers – were regularly kidnapped in Guatemala and southern Mexico, never to be seen again. A healthy baby was worth thousands of dollars in illegal adoptions, while older children were sold as servants or prostitutes. The Mayans who attacked the tourists were not so much deluded as afraid and concerned. When people live in frontier conditions, without secure social structures to rely on, they feel vulnerable, and make their own laws for their own circumstances, sometimes on the spot – and administer them with all the vigour of fear and self-defence. That is what the Mayans did.

It is lazy to attribute such tragedies to delusion. The real delusion is to think that people can live flourishingly without the mutual understanding, and therefore the safety, that comes from knowledge.

# Love

*To love a thing means wanting it to live.*

CONFUCIUS

It is no surprise that the feast dedicated to amorousness, St Valentine's Day, anticipates the onset of spring by a few weeks, as if to help rouse human sensibilities from their winter hibernation. Romance perfumes the air in spring; flowers appear for the express purpose of being bunched into lovers' tributes; chocolate manufacturers count their profits. Yet despite appearances, the kinds of love that are most significant to us are not those that fill novels and cinema screens. They are instead those we have for family, friends and comrades; for these are the loves that endure through the greater part of our lives, and give us our sense of self-worth, our stability, and the framework for our other relationships.

Romantic love, by contrast, is an episodic, usually short-lived, and often scorchingly vivid turbulence in our emotional histories. To judge by the attention it receives – not least in poetry and song, our parliaments for discussing the heart's essentials – it is one of life's profoundest experiences. Yet, paradoxically, the official line is that apart from a few experimental feints in early adulthood, love's true heights should only be experienced once, with lifelong bonding as the appropriate outcome. Anyone who claims to fall in love frequently is deemed irresponsible, and with some justification: for it is such a time-consuming, exhausting, ecstatic, painful, transforming business that it requires a long recovery – in some cases, indeed, whole lifetimes.

Sober folk claim that falling romantically in love is not a good way to get to know someone, for Stendhal's reason that we cloak the beloved in layers of crystal, and see a vision rather than a person for the whole period of our entrancement. On this view it is a delusional state, and the fact that it is short-lived is therefore good. Others think that romantic love is the only thing that allows us to burn through the layers that conventionally insulate people from one another, baring the soul of each to each, and making true communication possible – the kind that speaks the language of intimacy, not in words but in pleasures and desires.

This is far from the only difference of opinion about romantic love. Another debate rages over the question whether a propensity for romance is an essential human trait, or whether it is a social and historical construction, present in some periods and societies but absent from others. As this crucial question shows, romantic love is a scarcely understood phenomenon, not least because in modern times we have conflated it with features and expectations drawn from other kinds of love, which latter we have ceased to reflect upon as if their naturalness exempted them from consideration.

The Greeks had different words for love's different manifestations. They spoke of *agape*, altruistic love (in Latin *caritas*, which gives us – but with what a cold ring – our word 'charity'). They spoke of *ludus*, the playful affection of children and of casual lovers, and *pragma*, the understanding that exists between a long-established married couple. They spoke of *storge*, the love that grows between siblings or comrades-in-arms who have been through much together, and of *mania*, which is obsession. And they allied the latter with *eros* or sexual passion. They thought that love in all its forms was divinely inspired, in the case of the last by Aphrodite. But divine inspiration was not always welcome; manic eroticism, they said, was often inflicted as a punishment by the gods, and its unreasoning and distracting character interfered with what they most valued, namely intellect and courage. Both Plato and his pupil Aristotle, in their different ways, therefore placed friendship at the summit of emotional life, and consigned the love that craves bodily expression to a lower plane. For many Greeks *ataraxia*, which means 'peace of mind', was a great good that was always under threat from sexual love and its obsessions and jealousies, and that is why Sophocles applauded old age for releasing mankind from what he called the 'tyranny' of sexual desire.

In making these distinctions the Greeks showed an alertness to the fact that close relationships subserve a variety of ends. People need emotional satisfactions of many kinds, but chiefly those that stem from giving and receiving companionship, affection, and the affirmations of being liked and approved. People might occasionally enjoy solitude, but never loneliness; they need to feel connected and valued. All of the six loves of the Greeks are connections, and all but *mania* bring a sense of self-worth. In the Greek ideal, the best and strongest emotional bonds are those of friendship between equals. Romantic and erotic passion might be felt by a man for a boy or (not quite as acceptably) a woman, but this was a distraction, and too much of it was regarded as weakness.

The downgrading of relations with women had a long and unhappy influence in the West. In the Christian era – despite what is suggested by the medieval side-show of 'courtly love' as celebrated by troubadours – most marriages were economic and practical arrangements, with disparity in age, education and status making companionate marriage rare. It remained so until recent times: Thomas Hardy remarked that the reason men and women were unable to establish a genuine camaraderie even in his own day was that they associated with each other only in their pleasures, never in their labours.

In saying this, Hardy presaged a new ideal of love as a combination of romance and comradeship. This is something really new in Western civilisation. Both romance and friendship have always been ideals, but quite separately; and romance has taken very different forms at different times in history. Romantic-companionate love as we now view it received its definitive statement very recently indeed – in fact, at the hands of Hollywood in its golden age, between the 1930s and 1950s, in thousands of films of every genre. Of course, progress towards the acculturation of its ideals and norms had already begun in nineteenth-century literature, which established the now-familiar pattern: a couple fall romantically in love, and therefore commit themselves to an open-ended venture of exclusive cohabitation (marriage, or in more recent times its surrogates), with children in the garden and roses round the door. The standard denouement for a Victorian three-volume novel is the engagement of the hero and heroine in the last chapter. In Jane Austen earlier in the century, this terminus is reached by more reflective and sober means; not with high passion, not even with palpitations and breathlessness, save for a faint simulacrum of these in an early phase of each novel's development, to show that Elizabeth is not indifferent to Darcy, say, or Fanny to Thomas. The courtship of Emma and Mr Knightley is quintessential Austen: a matter of mind and morals, of character and decision.

Not so by the time of Hardy. Love here takes the form either of *mania* or mature sexual passion. In Hardy's prophecy of the newly emerging pattern, romance is not an end in itself but a step towards love of the other kinds – it becomes the porch to friendship, comradeship, the equal or near-equal partnership in life's adventure. 'When I look up, there you'll be, and when you look up, there I'll be,' says Gabriel Oak when he has gained

Bathsheba at last, in a summary that would have curdled the passion of a medieval troubadour for whom romance was all in all, and domesticity its nemesis.

In opposition to the view that romantic love was invented by the troubadours, some argue that it is a universal phenomenon. To claim this is to take sides in the debate between 'essentialists' and 'constructionists'. The former claim that romantic love is one of the four great, intrinsic, inescapable upheavals which define the human condition (the others are: being born, having children, and dying). The latter claim that although loving, in all its variety of objects and modes, is one of the central human emotions, how it is expressed is an historically determined matter. Both are right; for people have always fallen in love – which is to say become infatuated, desirous, obsessed in some degree; usually enough to lose sleep and to forget mundane tasks – but the expression of that state, the other forms of love it has been allied to, and the expectations nurtured by the parties to it, have been very variously conceived.

A Greek of classical antiquity might become passionate about a boy, but sex was not the only point, for the lover's task was to educate his beloved in military and political ways, and help him in the early part of his career. In the love stories told by Plutarch the point was to illustrate the destructiveness of sexual mania – showing, for example, how the girl Aristocleia, and in another tale the boy Actaeon, were physically torn apart by competing suitors trying to snatch them away. Shakespeare's lovers are also sexually manic; they can scarcely restrain themselves before a priest is found. Fielding and Richardson divide between them the uproarious tumble in the hay and the unremittingly threatened rape. Only with the increased education of women does the idea of a companionable love-life after erotic mania – indeed, initiated by it – come into focus, bringing other models to mind. Some are, once again, drawn from our earliest literature, as with Hector bidding his last farewell to Andromache – a scene touchingly drawn by Homer, who says the hero had to remove his helmet because its nodding plumes frightened his small son in Andromache's arms. Another example is the marriage of Penelope and Odysseus, the pattern of sustained fidelity. Modern sensibility took these comradely marriages and added them to romantic infatuation as its proper sequel, and a kind of emotional economy was born: the passion, the friendship, the companionship, the partnership, the nurturing and the needing, that were once offered by different relationships, could now come in a single handy package marked Spouse.

But the modern combination of romance and comradeship which has thus become our ideal often proves an unstable mixture. The obsessive character of romantic and erotic love cannot be understood without reference to sex, nor sex without reference to gender. Sex is about physical urges and action, gender is about social and psychological categories; their failure to pair neatly is a fruitful source of trouble. Companionate love does not exclude sexual love, but its premises and aims are very different. It is about the shared project of what is in effect a small business – which is what a home, a household, is – purchasing and budgeting and managing other (usually small) people, and transporting and storing things, saving and spending, and dealing with problems, like illnesses and burst pipes. Gender differences, shaped and enhanced by social pressures, were thought to provide an apt division of labour for these tasks: the husband goes out to work, the wife tends the children and home. But that division, and even the gender differences themselves, have in recent years been bitterly questioned, the more so because – against feminist hopes and principles – science seems to suggest that in the competition between nature and nurture the former has an insistent and irreducible role in determining sexual behaviour and gender characteristics. Irenic feminists say that this does not imply strict determinism: as rational beings we can adjust biology in the direction of justice, as we do when we control our aggression and selfishness. But others accuse science of bias, saying that it tries to conceal behind statistics an historical conspiracy against women. There is a measure of truth on both sides.

On one crucial point, gender determinism has seemed to some men to explain a major source of trouble in monogamy. It is, they claim, that heterosexual relationships have always been shaped in the interests of women, who control and ration the amount of sex in them. If this is true, it would be natural enough; women have to be mindful of the fact that, in the form of pregnancy and childbirth, their potential investment in sex is far greater than a man's. Safe and effective contraception is a very recent amenity, and old habits and needs die hard. It is for this reason, perhaps, that prostitution has been such an effective and long-standing friend to marriage, despite the hypocrisy that has usually surrounded it.

One measure of the generally unsuccessful nature of modern romantic-companionate love is the high rate at which the relationships based upon it fail. Divorce in the contemporary West runs at forty per cent – for unmarried couples the rate is higher – and many of the marriages that survive do so at a high cost of compromise by one or both partners. Blame is variously assigned, often to causes that come down to maleness. Some writers extrapolate from Freudian theory the view that men suffer a psychological 'wound' caused by separation from their mothers and their inability (in some writers, notably Sheila Sullivan in *Falling in Love*, their 'humiliating inability') to give birth and suckle. They claim that this alleged wound explains everything women deprecate in men, chief among them emotional immaturity, lack of communication about feelings, proneness to infidelity, latent or active misogyny, and – at the extreme – aggression. And they cite these, in turn, as what derails the project of equal romantic comradeship.

Even without its dubious Freudian underpinning, this is

improbable stuff, and no man will recognise what has been called 'the harsh anomie of masculine existence' as accounting for his behaviour in relationships. The problem, far more plausibly, lies elsewhere: in society's endeavours to manage, constrain, deny, re-route, prohibit, channel and manipulate sexual passion and romantic love. It is the dead hand of oppressive institutions – principally religions – which explains why love can be a problem: which it only is when rationed and starved, as it is in the 'family values' dispensation of monogamy and restrictive attitudes to sexual expression and variety. When rationed and starved, eros becomes destructive, prompting the moralisers, in their wisdom, to ration and starve it more. And thereby hangs many a long tale, as novels and films in their thousands show. If the modern experiment of romantic-companionate love is to succeed, it has to be freed from the institutional arrangements made centuries ago for a quite different kind of relationship – the practical-economic model of Christian monogamy – in which neither romance nor companionship was the most important thing.

It is both a pun and a truth to say that the subject of love has always been left to amateurs to explain. There is no science of love because it is too various and protean to fit a theory. People attempt love as climbers attempt Everest; they scramble along, and end by camping in the foothills, or half-way up, wherever their compromises leave them. Some get high enough to see the view, which we know is magnificent, for we have all glimpsed it in dreams. And that is what the feast of St Valentine is about: the dream of love. Life would be bitter indeed if the dream never became reality, or if the main experiences of love in our lives – *storge*, *pragma*, *ludus*, *agape* – were not enduring and stabilising enough to save us when the storms of *eros* and *mania* sweep over us – bringing bliss, and leaving havoc in their wake.

# Happiness

*Happiness depends on wisdom.*

SOPHOCLES

It has wisely been said that the search for happiness is one of the main sources of unhappiness in the world. Yet most people, if asked, would claim that happiness is the goal of life, and many would also claim that it justifies whatever choices bring it about. Is this really so? The questions 'Is happiness the appropriate goal of life?' and 'Is it true that happiness justifies the means to its attainment?' are connected, for if the answer to the first is 'Yes', then so is the answer to the second. Yet it is clear that the answer to the second is 'No': the fact that a serial killer is made happy by murdering people is no justification for his doing it.

This suggests that there are higher values in life than happiness, a result which at first sight seems wrong, priggish, or both, but which the point just made forces us to accept. And indeed, there are persuasive arguments to show that happiness, especially in its thin, modern sense of contentment or satisfaction, is not only a mistaken goal for life, but a misleading one.

First, though, it is necessary to dispose of an unpersuasive argument to the same conclusion, which says that happiness is not the point because life's aim lies beyond death, in some religiously conceived dispensation where those who now suffer and mourn will be rewarded. This was a useful belief for ruling elites to inculcate in their serfs and servants, but Nietzsche was not far wrong in dismissing it as 'slave morality', a comfort for history's victims – who should not have been seeking comfort, but redress.

The genuinely persuasive argument can be simply put. If life's goal really is happiness, then we can easily achieve it for all mankind by pouring a happiness-inducing chemical into the world's water supplies. So long as the supply is kept constant in perpetuity, we would not notice if things began to work inefficiently, and would not mind if disasters ensued, for the chemical would keep us smiling through.

The fact that this is a disagreeable idea shows that a state of happiness – of contentment or satisfaction – merely by itself is a negative state, a passive condition, which undermines things we value more: our striving and yearning, our improving and growing, our inventing and discovering. Of course, some of what goes under these adventurous names is apt to rebound on us, and often has in the past; but not as often as it has moved us forward as a species, bringing the intrinsic goods of knowledge and progress, despite the prices that have sometimes been paid for both.

It is true that happiness frequently, although not invariably, accompanies these endeavours, as smoke does fire; and when it does, it enhances them. But it is knowledge and progress which are primary, causing happiness as a side-effect; they are the goal, and the attendant happiness, when it comes, is a sign that they are being reached. But note that some people – wicked or insane ones – can be happy pursuing bad or mad ends, so the fact that happiness arises from the pursuit of goals is no guarantee that the goals are good ones.

Aristotle said that a life truly worth living is one that produces *eudaimonia*, the feeling of being 'watched over by a good angel' – an image he used figuratively, not in a literal religious sense.

Most translations of this term render it in English as 'happiness', the contemporary meaning of which entirely subverts the strong, active connotation of *eudaimonia* as well-doing and well-being, as living flourishingly. These positive attributes of the good life come, said Aristotle, from using humankind's highest faculty, Reason, to live wisely and justly, seeking the virtues which lie along the Golden Mean – courage as the mean between cowardice and rashness, generosity as the mean between selfishness and profligacy.

To the best of eudaimonic people Aristotle gave the label *megalopsychos*, meaning 'great-souled' (the Latin-derived term which translates Aristotle's word is 'magnanimous', from *magna anima*). Earlier times translated this term as 'gentleman', which will not now do because it has acquired class connotations. But it implies the idea that the goal of ethical life is multiple in character, involving respect and concern for others, and a duty to improve oneself and to use one's gifts for the sake not only of others but of the quality of one's own experience.

Such a life would indeed be 'happy' in an older sense of this term, the sense of Shakespeare and the eighteenth-century drafters of the American constitution, who specified 'life, liberty and the pursuit of happiness' as an inalienable right for each individual. In this older sense 'happy' means prosperous and flourishing – not in money terms, although that is not excluded, but in being fortunate in possessing such amenities of life as health, friendship and opportunities to enjoy the beauty of the world. In this usage, the word is far closer to Aristotle's original meaning.

The question of happiness is sometimes dramatised in the form of a question: 'Which would you rather be: an unhappy Socrates, or a happy pig?' Of course one would rather be a happy Socrates; but the point is that to have one's autonomy of mind, to be aware of the world, and to make one's own choices, is better by far than being passively happy at the expense of these

# PART II
## Foes and Fallacies

# Nationalism

*Nationalism is our form of incest, is our idolatry, is our insanity. 'Patriotism' is its cult.*

ERICH FROMM

Nationalism is an evil. It causes wars, its roots lie in xenophobia and racism, it is a recent phenomenon – an invention of the last few centuries – which has been of immense service to demagogues and tyrants but to no one else. Disguised as patriotism and love of one's country, it trades on the unreason of mass psychology to make a variety of horrors seem acceptable, even honourable. For example: if someone said to you, 'I am going to send your son to kill the boy next door' you would hotly protest. But only let him seduce you with 'Queen and Country!' 'The Fatherland!' 'My country right or wrong!' and you would find yourself permitting him to send all our sons to kill not just the sons of other people, but other people indiscriminately – which is what bombs and bullets do.

Demagogues know what they are about when they preach nationalism. Hitler said, 'The effectiveness of the truly national leader consists in preventing his people from dividing their attention, and keeping it fixed on a common enemy.' And he knew whom to appeal to: Goethe had long since remarked that nationalistic feelings 'are at their strongest and most violent where there is the lowest degree of culture'.

Nationalists take certain unexceptionable desires and muddle them with unacceptable ones. We individually wish to run our own affairs; that is unexceptionable. Most of us value the culture which shaped our development and gave us our sense of personal and group identity; that too is unexceptionable. But the nationalist persuades us that the existence of other groups and cultures somehow puts these things at risk, and that the only way to protect them is to see ourselves as members of a distinct collective, defined by ethnicity, geography, or sameness of language or religion, and to build a wall around ourselves to keep out 'foreigners'. It is not enough that the others are other; we have to see them as a threat – at the very least to 'our way of life', perhaps to our jobs, even to our daughters.

When Europe's overseas colonies sought independence, the only rhetoric to hand was that of nationalism. It had well served the unifiers of Italy and Germany in the nineteenth century (which in turn prepared the way for some of their activities in the twentieth century), and we see a number of the ex-colonial nations going the same way today.

The idea of nationalism turns on that of a 'nation'. The word is meaningless: all 'nations' are mongrel, a mixture of so many immigrations and mixings of peoples over time that the idea of ethnicity is largely comical, except in places where the boast has to be either that the community there remained so remote and disengaged, or so conquered, for the greater part of history, that it succeeded in keeping its gene pool 'pure' (a cynic might say 'inbred').

Much nonsense is talked about nations as entities: Emerson spoke of the 'genius' of a nation as something separate from its numerical citizens; Giraudoux described the 'spirit of a nation' as 'the look in its eyes'; other such meaningless assertions abound. Nations are artificial constructs, their boundaries drawn in the blood of past wars. And one should not confuse culture and nationality: there is no country on earth which is not home to more than one different but usually coexisting culture. Cultural heritage is not the same thing as national identity.

The blindness of people who fall for nationalistic demagoguery is surprising. Those who oppose closer relations in Europe, or who seek to detach themselves from the larger comities to which they belong, do well to examine the lessons of such tragedies as the Balkans conflicts, or – the same thing writ larger – Europe's bloody history in the twentieth century.

# Racism

*Racism is on its deathbed — the question is, how costly will racists make the funeral?*

MARTIN LUTHER KING

Almost everywhere one looks among present societies, race and racism make angry welts and deep wounds on the body politic. It is an irony that although racism is a reality, and a harsh one, race itself is a fiction. The concept of race has no genetic or biological basis. All human beings are closely related to one another, and at the same time each human being is unique. Not only is the concept of race entirely artificial, it is new; yet in its short existence it has, like most lies and absurdities current among us, done a mountain of harm.

The first classification of humans into races was mooted by Linnaeus, who recognised it as a mere convenience with no basis in nature. He employed the same criteria as in his botanical classifications, namely, outward appearance, giving rise later to the simplistic typing of all humans into 'Caucasoid', 'Negroid' and 'Mongoloid'. But advances in genetics have demolished such taxonomies, by taking DNA as the criterion of classification. Linnaeus's system says that one of Buddhism's holy plants, the lotus, is related to the water lily; DNA comparison says it is related to London's familiar and beloved plane tree.

In human terms DNA analysis dismantles the idea of race completely. 'Race has no basic biological reality,' says Professor

Jonathan Marks of Yale University; 'the human species simply doesn't come packaged that way.' Rather, race is a social, cultural and political concept based on superficial appearances and historical conditions, largely those arising from encounters with other peoples as Europe developed a global reach, with the slavery and colonialism that followed.

It was not only Linnaeus who knew that 'race' is a fiction. In the mid-nineteenth century E. A. Freeman famously discredited the whole of idea of 'community of blood', as did Ashley Montagu in the mid-twentieth century. Even Hitler knew it, despite making the concept central: 'I know perfectly well ... that in a scientific sense there is no such thing as race,' he said, 'but I as a politician need a concept which enables the order which has hitherto existed on historic bases to be abolished and an entirely new and antihistoric order enforced and given an intellectual basis ... And for this purpose the concept of races serves me well ... With the concept of race, National Socialism will carry its revolution abroad and recast the world.'

All human beings have the same ancestors. Human history is a short one; it is less than a quarter of a million years long, with the first migrations from Africa beginning half that time ago. The physical diversity of human populations today is purely a function of geographical accidents of climate and the isolation of wandering bands. The distinctions which have since been drawn between peoples are therefore arbitrary and superficial, even those relating to skin colour – for as a moment's attention shows, there is simply no such thing as 'white', 'black' or 'yellow' people; there are people with many shades and types of skin, making no difference to any other aspect of their humanity save what the malice of others can construct.

To advance beyond racism one has to advance beyond race. But that goal is not helped by what Sartre called 'anti-racist racism', as with the Black Power movement and its cognates. It is understandable that communities which suffer prejudice and abuse should shelter behind a protective assumed identity; but identities grow rigid and become a source of new pieties, new excuses to repay evil with evil – and thereby indirectly entrench the very idea that lies at the root of the problem.

Racism will end when individuals see others only in individual terms. 'There are no "white" or "coloured" signs on the graveyards of battle,' said John F. Kennedy; and there is a significant moral in that remark.

# Speciesism

*Animals are not brethren, they are not underlings; they are
other nations, caught with ourselves in the net of life and
time.*

HENRY BESTON

A striking fact now rendered familiar, even platitudinous, by
the triumphs of recent genetic science is how closely all
living things are related. Humans share more than half their
genes with worms and fruit-flies, and almost all their genes
with chimpanzees. Yet this intimate familyhood of life does not
stop people from spearing worms onto fish-hooks, or testing
drugs on chimpanzees. Nothing surprising there, you might say,
given the way humans treat humans; in the face of gas chambers,
racism, war and other avocations, what chance has a monkey
or a cow?

There are lessons to be learned from the way humans justify
their treatment of animals – not least of those evolutionarily
closest to them – namely, the apes. Apes, especially gorillas,
have long been demonised in film and literature. Their simi-
larity to us is used not as proof of kindred, but as a means of
symbolising the supposed bestiality within us. Thus when Dr
Jekyll drinks his potion he exposes a mythologised savage inheritance; his hands grow hairy, his brow beetles, his teeth enlarge:
he becomes a horrifying gorilla-man.

If it is not violence it is stupidity which marks the ape,
betokened by tree-swinging, armpit-scratching and gibbering.

You insult a person if you call him an ape. Yet apes are intelligent, inquisitive, affectionate and sociable, with capacities for suffering and grief that match our own, and with a grave beauty and dignity which recalls Schopenhauer's remark that 'There is one respect in which brutes show real wisdom when compared to us – I mean their quiet, placid enjoyment of the present moment.'

There is a parallel between our excuses for maltreating apes and those for maltreating fellow humans. We locate a difference that we find threatening, or that we despise; we thereby make the other fully Other, so that we can close the door of the moral community against him, leaving him outside where our actions cannot be judged by the same standards as apply within. Racism and speciesism are thus the same thing – they are myths about who belongs and who is alien.

In their book *The Great Ape Project* published some years ago, Paola Cavalieri and Peter Singer entered a plea for humankind to 'admit our fellow Great Apes – the chimpanzees, gorillas and orangutans – to the same moral community as ourselves, thereby according them rights to life, to liberty, and to protection against torture – especially the kind of torture inflicted in the name of scientific research.' In the face of the genetic and behavioural evidence, there is no good reason why the moral respect and consideration that applies between humans should not apply between humans and apes. But note: the moment that the boundaries of morality are extended in this way, there is no obvious place to stop. All animate nature comes within the purview of ethics; and that, arguably, is as it should be.

The world divides into vegetarians and those that eat them. Thoreau wrote, 'I have no doubt that it is a part of the destiny of the human race, in its gradual improvement, to leave off eating animals, as surely as the savage tribes have left off eating each other.' There are plenty who argue that it is not immoral to eat a cow, especially if it has lived well beforehand. Lovers of cats and dogs would think it cruel to eat their pets, though, and once again the reason is the boundary: cats and dogs, horses and even hamsters, have become quasi-citizens of the human world, and our treatment of them is premised on the same kind of concern for their interests as we show to other humans. We would not crowd dogs into a closed lorry as we do sheep when they are sent on long export journeys; that is a happy fact. But it is an unhappy fact that we crowd sheep into lorries, for sheep can suffer thirst and panic just as dogs – and humans – do.

Humanity's record with animals is poor. 'We have enslaved the rest of the animal creation,' wrote Dean Inge, 'and have treated our distant cousins in fur and feathers so badly that beyond doubt, if they were able to formulate a religion, they would depict the Devil in human form.' Some think that sentimental do-goodery over animals is a distraction from more significant moral matters. Perhaps; but a person's integrity is never more fully tested than when he has power over a voiceless creature; and the route from pulling wings off flies to committing crimes against humanity is not a notably circuitous one.

# Hate

*Hatred is a sentiment that leads to the extinction of values.*
ORTEGA Y GASSET

Such emotions as guilt, shame and pride usually have oneself as their object, or things one closely identifies with, such as family or (for patriots) country. They are obviously self-referential feelings. Such emotions as love, hatred, contempt and pity, which are directed outwards, towards other people or things, appear not to be self-referential at first, but in an indirect way they are. The reason is that most emotions involve beliefs: if you are ashamed, you believe that you have done something that deserves the contempt of others; if you feel pity, you believe that the object of your compassion is suffering in a way that merits your concern. In both cases you remain in the equation, as a point of reference, and as the sensibility stirred by the beliefs in question.

This is especially true of hatred, which is dislike and antipathy inflamed to a high degree and inspired by beliefs which stimulate a set of other emotions in the hater, chief among them fear, ignorance, jealousy, anger and disgust. But note that all these emotions, and especially the first three, are about the hater; thus hating says more about haters than what they hate. It shows weakness, for it is a crude emotion which turns fears and anxieties outward to fix them on something else. When one dislikes a person on good grounds – because he is provenly dishonest, malevolent, or treacherous, say – the appropriate reaction is disdain, and a withholding of social courtesies. Someone truly contemptible does not merit the energy that stronger emotions require. And as La Rochefoucauld observed, 'When our hatred is too keen it puts us below those we hate,' which is an allied point.

Moralisers – the people who seek to impose on everyone else their own timid conception of morality, usually in the form of the historically recent and painfully failed 'family values' ethos – are in a fair way to being haters of anyone who thinks differently from them. Certainly the ingredients are there: fear of different choices and lifestyles, ignorance about their interests and experiences, jealousy of their freedom from the disciplines that the moralists impose on themselves, disgust and anger at what others do: these are the ingredients of hate which, when wrapped in the pious rhetoric of conventional morality, breed repression, illiberality, and narrowness. A key lies in the fact that the views which moral conservatives try to impose on others are often an expression of what they most fear in themselves: 'if you hate a person,' Herman Hesse remarked, 'you hate something in him that is part of yourself.'

As the Nazis showed in their attitude to Jews and also to homosexuals, gypsies and Slavs, hatred is at its apogee when applied to groups, whose individual members therefore come to be viewed as mere units, defined only by their group membership and damned for the label it bears. It is easy to hate a label; it is almost impossible to hate an individually known human being. One might dislike an individual and feel contempt for him, but the blanket impulse of hatred, so deep and negative that it reveals nothing so clearly as the hater's own emotional inadequacy, is a different matter. Moreover, it is easier to hate a group as a member of an opposing group, for hatred is a natural emotion for the mass mind, along with devotion and other large, shapeless hysterias.

It is worth remembering that hatred always has small beginnings. 'It is enough that one man hate another,' wrote Sartre, 'for hate to gain, little by little, all mankind.'

seek redress on their own; justice cannot be a matter of private enterprise. Recognition of this fact from the earliest times led to the building of institutions of justice, culminating – in mature societies – in laws, with officers to oversee their proper application, and with due form and process as a protection against whatever forces might pervert their functioning.

A system of justice can be seen as a well-meaning human endeavour (describing it as such acknowledges the imperfection of all human creations) to provide an objective and impartial means of redressing wrong, whether against individuals or the collective. Because the justice system is constituted by the collective, from which it gets its authority, it acts as the collective's agent, and carries out its desire for justice wherever required and possible. Revenge is only one part of the aim, if it is part of the aim at all – some think the aim should exclusively be rehabilitation, never retribution – and this downgrading of revenge is appropriate in a mature state of society, where the fundamental idea of the implicit contract between its members, and between each of them and all the others, is to live by the rules for the sake of all-round mutual benefit. When individual members of society flout the rules, they accept the agreed sanctions for doing so; but that is not a case of society taking revenge, properly speaking, so much as redressing the balance of relationships and repairing the wrong done to them.

Desire for revenge is most dangerous when felt by individuals additionally oppressed by fear, anger, and a sense of impotence in the face of perceived injustice. Most of the world's flashpoints are thickly wreathed in such combustible vapours. When someone who seems to have every reason in the world to seek revenge – Nelson Mandela, say – does not do so, the example set is extraordinary and impressive. 'No revenge is more honourable than the one not taken,' says the Spanish proverb. There is nobility in forbearance, and it expresses a desire for something far greater and grander than revenge, namely peace, a future, and an end to the festering hatreds and hurts which poison life. It takes magnanimity – that impressive word Anglicised from *magna anima* meaning 'great soul' – to rise above revenge. Magnanimity is always in short supply, but it is the main ingredient in everything that makes the world a better place, and the only antidote to the rage for revenge which, without fail, always makes bad things worse.

# Intemperance

*Intemperance is the physician's provider.*

PUBLILIUS SYRUS

A night of alcohol-assisted celebration, especially of a major event, might leave one feeling a trifle rough-edged, or worse: allergic to light and sound, averse to the thought of food, intolerant even of the simplest and mildest forms of human intercourse. Such are the wages of intemperance. There is a trick in the nature of some things, but especially of those two wild horsemen, alcohol and merriment, that urges one on just when one has already gone too far. That is the secret of excess: it happens when it has already happened. 'Since the creation of the world,' wrote William Garrison, 'there has been no tyrant like intemperance, and no slaves so cruelly treated as his.'

There is a school of thought which applauds intemperance because of its educational value. 'The road of excess leads to the palace of wisdom,' said Blake. Not only is it exhilarating in itself, but it has the salutary effect of preventing moderation becoming a habit. It would be a sad individual who never overstepped a limit to see what the world looks like from the other side. What do they know of sobriety, it might be asked, who only sobriety know? It is surely not too paradoxical to claim that excess, in moderation, keeps one's sense of perspective, and has a cathartic effect, flushing clogged-up conventionalities out of one's sensibility. By 'moderate excess' I do not mean a daring half-pint over the normal; I mean the occasional bender, but not every night.

But there are darker thoughts. Christopher Fry aptly noted that 'Indulgences, not fulfilment, is what the world permits us,' and there is a deep truth there. All instruments of excess are distractions; the most they teach us, when they teach us anything, is the value of their absence. People aspire to possess things of value, and yearn for superlatives in experience; enough intoxicant gives the illusion of both. But illusions carry one in a direction exactly opposite to the desired reality. This is not a moralising point, for anyone is entitled to substitute a dream that can be readily and quickly invoked for a reality which is hard, long, and uncertain in the getting. It is just that everyone who has visited the reality knows how much better it is, in its own right, than any blurred and temporary simulacrum can hope to be. The messenger who brings that news is always in danger of being shot for an elitist, but the truth is not his fault.

Epicurus is the philosopher who taught that pleasure is the highest good, pain the greatest evil; his teaching is epitomised in the injunction to pursue the former and avoid the latter. He thereby gives us our adjective for those who like the good life, and tread at least close to the margins of excess: 'Epicurean'. It comes as a surprise to most, therefore, when they learn that he drank only water and said that life's highest pleasure is discussing philosophy with friends under a shady tree. Yet he not only saw the value of intemperance, but understood its more interesting sources: 'We would have no reason to find fault with the intemperate,' he wrote, 'if the things that produce their pleasures were really able to drive away their fears about death, and pain, and to teach them the limits of their desires.' What gave him sorrow is that those supposed pleasures do the opposite.

An old French proverb says that 'It is only the first bottle that is expensive.' In this is the head and foot of all the wisdom about intemperance that anyone needs, or perhaps – the morning after a night before – is willing to bear.

One can be intemperate in many ways, but as the foregoing remarks suggest, it is most often applied to the use of alcohol and other intoxicants. It should not be surprising that people choose to mark significant occasions by getting intoxicated – which is to say: by inducing temporary but often profound changes in their usual selves – for history teaches that people have always had special reasons for doing so. Past societies regarded it (and some still do) as a way of communing with the gods, and as revealing people to one another and themselves. It gave people a holiday from themselves, and from the usual constraints of life. Indeed, the importance of allowing people to have "moral holidays" was so widely recognised that all dispensations had their licensed feast days and seasons of revelry, even – as with the feast of the Lord of Misrule – allowing the social world to be turned upside down for a day, with the king serving the clown.

Alcohol was not the only door to divinity or self-release. Most basic forms of drugs have long been familiar to mankind, and their remarkable properties gave them a central and valued role in community life. The substances capable of effecting such transformations belonged to the same ancient pharmacopoeia as medicine, and when austerer religions started to fear their anarchic power, the people who produced them came to be demonised – into witches, wizards, and devil's familiars. As societies have grown more numerous and complex, so the effort to control the availability and use of intoxicants has grown – the chief reason being that their effects make people ungovernable.

As the name implies, an intoxicant is a substance that poisons the human body, and by doing so alters states of feeling and perception. The brain tries to defend itself against the disruptive effect of most chemicals by shielding itself behind a 'blood-brain barrier', but intoxicants are precisely those substances capable of penetrating the barrier, thereby disturbing the normal, delicate, chemical marinade of the brain and disrupting its functions. One advantage of alcohol is that its effects are proportional to quantity; a little alcohol serves as a relaxing social lubricant, helping fellow guests warm to one another, but (even at legal levels) making the imbiber a menace behind a steering-wheel. Larger quantities vanquish his muscular control and inhibitions; and quantities larger still can kill him. 'The vine bears three kinds of grapes,' wrote Anacharsis, 'the first of pleasure, the second of intoxication, the third of disgust.'

Admonishers in the days before drink-driving (a kind of murder waiting to happen) focused on alcohol's indiscretion. 'What a sober man has in his heart,' says the Danish proverb, 'the drunk has on his lips.' They also pointed at the destructive effect of systematic drinking on family life and individual health. Alcohol dependency was then thought to be an exclusively moral failure, but is now recognised as a social and – more to the point – medical problem. It is a measure of alcohol's centrality to life that it has resisted (in the days of Prohibition, at enormous cost) every effort to criminalise it, unlike other drugs. Alcohol marks the limits of government, one might say.

Certainly it marks the limits of self-government. 'Drink never made a man better,' says Dunne's sage Mr Dooley, 'but it has made many a man think he was.' The observation applies generally. The self-same Mr Dooley held that many couples would never have arrived at the altar together had it not been for drink. 'It's the wise man who stays home when he's drunk,' said Euripides, perhaps thinking the same thing.

But these wary remarks will influence few party-goers and revellers, who will prefer Lord Byron's view that 'Man, being reasonable, must get drunk; the best of life is but intoxication.' Who could disagree – if he meant intoxication by art, letters, music and love?

# Depression

*One cloud is enough to eclipse all the sun.*

THOMAS FULLER

Depression caused by winter's dark days is called 'seasonal affective disorder', the apt and expressive acronym for which is SAD. In the great majority of cases relief is afforded by a daily half-hour exposure to bright light. Most SAD sufferers are women, and the complaint seems to be genetic. Ordinary light bulbs do not help; the light must be intense and broad-spectrum (but not full-spectrum, because harmful ultraviolet is best excluded). The theory is that melatonin, which regulates sleep and mood, is over-produced by prolonged darkness, and broad-spectrum light suppresses it. One can likewise alter one's internal clock in jet-lag by adjusting melatonin levels.

SAD is a winter disease – 'See, Winter comes to rule the varied year,/Sullen and Sad,' wrote James Thompson. It is also a geographical one: not surprisingly, far more people suffer from it in Alaska than Florida, but the reason is not solely the number of photons available in each place. The ancient Egyptians saw their god every day and felt his power on their backs – Ra, the Sun – and one has only to compare the giant oranges of Florida with their non-existence in Alaska to see what such a god can do. With light comes warmth, loose clothing, freer movement, more exercise, and the avocations of summer: sea, and sails dotted upon it, the cry of gulls, ice cream, bikinis, sand between the toes: in short, everything calculated to cheer one up. The contrast with dark, bleak mornings and the onset of night in mid-afternoon, all horizons closed and everything muffled, could not be sharper.

'Let us love winter, for it is the spring of genius,' said Pietro Aretino; and only an Italian could say such a thing. In the far north, where humans first undoubtedly went not for love of cold and dark but to escape the danger of other humans, the sunless months are long and many. Suppose it to be true that humanity's first home was hot, strongly lit, riotous with vivid tropical colours and luscious scents; what deep instincts are forced to lie dormant in a silent world of snow, where night never ends? Jacques Maritain says, 'What makes man most unhappy is to be deprived not of that which he had, but of that which he did not have, and did not really know.' That makes SAD a genetic yearning for Eden, which paleoanthropology tells us lay in Africa.

Clinical depression – as opposed to the minor fluctuations of mood for which Dodie Smith bracingly recommends 'noble deeds and hot baths' as the best cures – is a serious illness, requiring careful and sympathetic treatment. SAD is a form of clinical depression, although happily for sufferers, its cause is clear and its cure easy for most. But between the normal ups and downs and the serious medical condition there is a state which, inevitably and appropriately, visits every inhabitant of the human condition. The Greek tragedians, in characteristic Eeyore vein, are apt to overstate it: 'Fate finds for every man/ His share of misery,' Euripides says; but the state in question is not misery or grief, but a kind of melancholy, in which it is possible to feel and understand things not available in other moods – for our moods are like tunings on the wireless, picking up truths at different frequencies, so that if we do not know the gamut of human feelings, neither can we know the gamut of truth.

Such melancholy is fitted to the fact that life offers causes for regret, that happiness is not always the point, and that there is enough hardship and struggle to go round, but not enough of the good things; and reflection on these useful insights is a check on thoughtlessness and self-satisfaction – what the Russians expressively call *poshlost* – which threaten to make one live in banal fashion. So a little depression is good at times, in any season.

# Christianity

*Christians have burnt each other, quite persuaded*
*That all the Apostles would have done as they did.*

LORD BYRON

Christianity is an oriental religion whose irruption into the classical world overwhelmed it and changed the course of its development. It is fruitless to speculate how the history of the West might have proceeded if Christianity had expired, after a short time, as merely another version of that common Middle Eastern theme – from Egyptian mythology to the Orphic rites – of the dying and reviving god. But we can make a guess, as follows.

For one thing, Plato's and Aristotle's academies in Athens would not have been suppressed in AD 529 on the grounds of their 'pagan' teachings. The delicate irony attaching to this occurrence is that their suppressor, Justinian, named the great church he built in Constantinople 'The Church of the Holy Wisdom'. For another, there would have been no Christians to put a stop to the Olympic games in AD 393 because they disliked the athletes' nudity. *Gymnos*, from which our 'gymnastics' comes, means 'naked'.

Apologists might say that without the accident of Christianity's becoming the official religion of the Roman Empire, we would be without the glorious Annunciations and Crucifixions of Renaissance art. But in balance with the sanguinity of Christian history – its crusades, Inquisitions, religious wars, drowned witches, oppressive morals and hostility to sex – this seems a minor loss. In place of Annunciations we would have more depictions of Apollo Pursuing Daphne, the Death of Procris, Diana Bathing, and the like. By almost any standards, apart from the macabre and gloomy ones of Puritan sensibility, an Aphrodite emerging from the Paphian foam is infinitely more life-enhancing an emblem than a gloomy Deposition from the Cross.

The religious attitude is marked by a robust refusal to take things at face value if inconvenient. Take this passage from the Book of Samuel – in its King James robes, a wonderful piece of prose – and ask how attractive it makes religion seem: 'Then said Samuel, "Bring ye hither to me Agag, King of the Amalekites." And Agag came to him delicately. And Agag said, "Surely the bitterness of death is passed." And Samuel said, "As thy sword hath made women childless, so shall thy mother be childless among women." And Samuel hewed Agag in pieces before the Lord in Gilgal.'

If the mincing of Agag wrought divine pleasure, then it is surely the Prometheus of Goethe who has the gods' measure: 'I know nothing more wretched under the sun than you, ye gods! Scantily you feed your majesty on sacrifices and the breath of prayer; and you would starve if beggars and children were not hopeful fools.'

Leslie Stephen pointed out that while religion flourishes, ethical enquiry is restricted to casuistry, that is, the science of interpreting divine commands. The ultimate justification of these rests on a logical fallacy with a forbidding Latin name, the *argumentum ad baculum*, which can be explained as follows. The religious reply to the moral sceptic's question, 'Why should I behave in such-and-such a way?' is simply 'Because God requires it of you.' But this is merely a polite way of saying, 'Because you'll be punished if you don't.' This is what the *argumentum ad baculum* comes down to: the use of a threat, literally 'an appeal to force'. But a threat is never a logical justification for acting one way rather than another. If there exists a deity with the punitive vengefulness of the Judaeo-Christian variety, then it might be prudent to obey it, and thus avoid the flames of hell; but the threat of punishment is not a principled reason for obedience.

Religious apologists claim that our motive for acting morally should not be the threat of divine vengeance, but love of God and our fellow man. But this is pious camouflage, however well meant. For in the religious view, if someone chooses not to act on the prompting of such affections, or fails to feel them at all, he is not therefore excused exile in the place of wailing and gnashing of teeth. He will suffer the fate of the fig-tree which, we are told in a pre-environmentally-sensitive biblical text, was blasted for bearing no fruit out of season.

A secular moralist would say: If love (in the sense of the Greek term *agape*: in Latin, *caritas*, hence 'charity') is the reason for being moral, what relevance does the existence or non-existence of a deity have? Why can we not be prompted to the ethical life by our own charitable feelings? The existence of a god adds nothing to our moral situation, other than an invisible policeman who sees what we do (even in privacy and under cover of night), and a threat of post-mortem terrors if we misbehave. Such additions are hardly an enrichment of the moral life, since the underpinning they offer consists of fear and threats of punishment: which is exactly what, among other things, the moral life seeks to free us from.

This prompts the question: Why are the churches given a privileged – almost, indeed, an exclusive – position in the social debate about morality, when they are arguably the least competent organisations to have it?

If this claim seems paradoxical, it is because we have become used to giving, as if by reflex, a platform to churchmen when moral dilemmas arise. This has come about in an odd way. The churches have always been obsessed with a small range of human activities, mainly those associated with sexuality. They have always sought to channel and constrain sexual behaviour, and it is their vociferous complaining about human turpitude on this score that has somehow made them authorities on moral matters in general. But it can easily be shown that they are either largely irrelevant to genuine questions of morality, or are positively anti-moral.

In modern developed societies approval is given to such values as personal autonomy, achievement in earning a living, providing for a family, saving against a rainy day, and meriting rewards for success in one's career. Christian morality says the exact opposite. It tells people to take no thought for the morrow – 'consider the lilies of the field, which neither reap nor spin', and to give all their possessions to the poor. It warns that it is easier for a camel to go through a needle's eye than for a well-off person to enter heaven. It preaches complete submission to the will of a deity, which is the opposite of personal autonomy and responsibility. Such a morality is wholly at odds with the norms and practices of contemporary society. Most people simply ignore the contradiction between such views and today's ethos, and the churches keep quiet about it. But if anyone bothered to examine what a Christian – or indeed any religious – morality demanded, he would be amazed by its diametric opposition to what is regarded as normal and desirable now, yet he would see – independently of whether it is the Christian or the contemporary morality which is 'right' – the reason why the former is irrelevant to the latter.

But religious morality is not merely irrelevant, it is anti-moral. The great moral questions of the present age are those about human rights, war, poverty, the vast disparities between rich and poor, the fact that somewhere in the third world a child dies every two and a half seconds because of starvation or remediable disease. The churches' obsessions over pre-marital sex and whether divorced couples can remarry in church appears contemptible in the light of this mountain of human suffering and need. By distracting attention from what really counts, and focusing it on the minor and anyway futile attempt to get people to conduct their personal lives only in ways the church permits, harm is done to the cause of good in the world.

But religion is not only anti-moral, it can often be immoral. Elsewhere in the world, religious fundamentalists and fanatics incarcerate women, mutilate genitals, amputate hands, murder, bomb and terrorise in the name of their faiths. It is a mistake to think that our own Western milk-and-water clerics would never conceive of doing likewise; it is not long in historical terms since Christian priests were burning people at the stake if they did not believe that wine turns to blood when a priest prays over it, and that the earth sits immovably at the universe's centre, or – more to the present point – since they were whipping people and slitting their noses and ears for having sex outside marriage, or preaching that masturbation is worse than rape because at least the latter can result in pregnancy. To this day adulterers are stoned to death in certain Muslim countries; if the priests were still on top in the once-Christian world, who can say it would be different?

Because so much religious energy is devoted to controlling sexual behaviour, either by disallowing it (or thoughts or representations of it) other than in strictly limited cir-cumstances, or by preventing the amelioration of its con-sequences once it has happened, we have the spectacle of righteous people writing letters of complaint about televised nudity, while from the factory next door tons of armaments are exported to regions of the world gripped by poverty and civil war. With such examples and contrasts, religion has very little to offer moral debate.

Defenders of religion are quick to point out that church-based charities do much good at home and abroad. And so they do; their work, like that of secular aid organisations and charities, is welcome and needed. But three thoughts press. One is that secular organisations are based on humanitarian promptings, and need no appeal to beliefs about supernatural agencies to explain their source or give them their impetus. The second is that no secular organisation is going to use overt or covert means to claim some of those they help for a particular world-view – Roman Catholicism or some other denomination or faith. And thirdly, the sticking-plaster of charitable concern shown by religious organisations does little to compensate for the massive quantum of suffering with which religion has burdened the world historically, and which is by far the larger part of the fruits by which we know them.

No doubt the churches are as entitled as any other interest group to have their say on matters that fall within their range of concerns; but they are an interest group nonetheless, with highly tendentious views, and big axes to grind. Asking them to take an especially authoritative line on moral matters is like asking the fox to set the rules for fox-hunting. Churchmen are people with avowedly ancient supernatural beliefs who rely on moral casuistry which is 2000 years out of date; it is extraordinary that their views should be given any precedence over those that could be drawn from the richness of thoughtful, educated, open-minded opinion otherwise available in society.

When a bishop says that the interests of morality are best served by setting aside considerations of religion and God, it is appropriate to sit up and take notice. The bishop in question is the Right Reverend Richard Holloway, Bishop of Edinburgh and Primus of the Church of Scotland – aptly so entitled, as it happens, as a frequent cooker-up of controversy, and one who sets fire to much debate in the Anglican Communion and elsewhere for his liberal views on sex, homosexuals, drugs and abortion. These very issues form the focus of his book *Godless Morality*, in which he makes a plea, liberal in inspiration, for what he calls a 'morality of consent'. Despite the secular connotations of the book's title, the bishop's plea is chiefly aimed at countering moral conservatism in the Christian churches; to already convinced secular liberals his arguments have long been familiar.

The first source of dismay for any members of the Bishop's flock will be his argument that moral debate does better without God. One reason, he says, is that unbelieving but principled people are insulted by the claim that we have to be religious to be moral, and moreover the history of religion's many and scarlet crimes against humanity makes that claim profoundly suspect. But his chief reason is the excellent one that an ethic should stand on its own feet, recommending itself to reason and goodwill, needing no support from divine threats of retribution to force compliance. Holloway argues that morality once took its cue from social arrangements in which authority was a matter of command from above – for example, from a king – but that times have changed: the loss of tradition and authority in society, and the passing of an unjust dispensation in which the female half of humanity was deprived of full human status, means that 'command morality' has to be replaced by 'consent morality', in which moral considerations are sensitive to the often irreconcilable pluralism of modern life, and to the demands, sexual and otherwise, of Nature in our make-up.

One immediate effect of detaching morality from religion, Holloway shows, is a grateful deliverance from the concept of sin. Sin is disobedience to God; morality is about relationships, responsibility and concern. Religion deals in absolutes; but in the wide variousness of the human condition there are no absolutes, only competing goods and desires. One of Holloway's key points is that this fact makes a turn to 'consent morality' indispensable. And once we make that turn, we find a better and more humane way to think about the central foci of moral anxiety in contemporary society – chief among them sex, drugs, abortion, euthanasia, and human fertility.

In arguing for a more liberal and permissive attitude to each of these matters Holloway employs the idea of 'ethical jazz', by which he means 'playing it by ear' in dealing with individual dilemmas as they arise. He insists, absolutely rightly, that when you know the special circumstances of any given case, you are far more likely to be sympathetic than when opposing an alleged form of immorality as a type. In a nice touch he characterises his view thus: 'let's motor; but let's keep the brakes in good working order'. This summarises what he also calls his 'middle way': prohibition of drugs is counter-productive, but complete licence would be harmful; abortion is not always murder; fertility treatment should be welcomed as helpful to those in genuine need of it.

Among the Bishop's views the most welcome is his positive attitude towards homosexuality, and the most interesting is his belief that contemporary sexual mores do not signify a deepening of immorality.

He holds the former view because he is a churchman who wishes the church to be open to all, to include rather than to alienate. In line with this view he often champions the cause of gays and lesbians in the church, and he repeats the case here.

His view about sex is more complex. He thinks that what young people call 'shagging' – viz. opportunistic, casual, recreational sex – does not interfere with the belief held by the same young people that commitment to a relationship means sexual fidelity and monogamy for the long term. And he thinks (adopting their terminology) that shagging is not outlawed by the Bible, which not only abounds in it but in forms of it (such as incest) which have completely lost the respectability they seem to have enjoyed in the days of Judah and Lot. Moreover, he blames Gnosticism for Christianity's unhealthy and deeply hostile attitude towards sex, implying that the New Testament is not much less tolerant than parts of the Old Testament in these respects.

Now, this interesting view is the precise point at which problems with the Bishop's stance arise. As mentioned, his book is really an argument with Christian conservatives; his target audience is the flock of Christians wavering between his own liberal line and the conservatives' more austere and traditional view. Truly secular liberals in moral matters would find nothing original or surprising about the Bishop's position, which they would regard as straightforward, humane common sense. By issuing a polemic against the conservatives Holloway demonstrates the continuing strength of their position. They say that the church's truths are for all time, and that when it is written 'to lie with a man as with a woman is an abomination' and 'women must cover their heads and keep silent in church ... and must obey their husbands', these injunctions are marmoreal: disobey them and you are punished in hell. So Holloway has to say that the Bible is allegorical, was written for the social circumstances of its time, and anyway has no single, stable point of view from which a morality can be deduced. Holloway has thus to be a trimmer to adapt the church to modern times; his book is proof of the fact that religion has to be reinvented practically out of recognition if it is going to stay alive and speak to changing times.

Moreover, in trying to save sex from Christianity, Holloway is not entirely ingenuous in unloading the blame on Gnosticism. St Paul, and the Church Fathers with their slavish acceptance of Platonism's depreciation of the body at the expense of the soul, have far more to do with it. Christian fear of sex and correlative hatred of women runs deep, almost as deep as the sexual impulse itself in human nature; which is why the former seems increasingly irrelevant as the latter surfaces into the fresh air of common sense and scientific understanding.

# Sin

*Oh Lord, it is not the sins I have committed that I regret but those which I have had no opportunity to commit.*

GHALIB

In its efforts to control a life-threatening practice whose effects are a degenerative progression from weakness and nervous exhaustion through blindness to madness and death, the medical profession once prescribed chloral hydrate, potassium bromide and opium for onset cases, and for more serious cases digitalis, strychnine ('which may be safer when mixed with small doses of arsenic,' said one helpful practitioner) and orally administered hydrochloric acid. If this did not work, the next resort was the application of leeches to the thighs, blistering or scalding of the peritoneum or genitals, and application of electric currents to those organs. When all else failed, surgical intervention in the form of infibulation of the prepuce, circumcision, castration or clitoridectomy was indicated. To ensure that the practice in question would not begin at all, parents were advised to stitch the sleeves of their children's nightgowns to the bedcovers, or tie their ankles to opposite sides of the crib, or make them wear a thick towel or nappy.

The practice, of course, was masturbation, regarded with horror and dread by moralists and medical men from the eighteenth to the early twentieth century. In some circles the belief that masturbation is enfeebling and causes a variety of nervous and sexual disorders persists. The origin of this lunacy was religious, and principally Christian, dread of sex and sexual feelings, which in the medieval and Renaissance world focused on melancholia, leprosy, syphilis and plague as divine punishments for sin and especially sexual sin, and in modern times (that is, from the seventeenth century onwards) expressed itself in theories about the medical dangers of any form of excess, 'perversion' or 'self-abuse'. A rather simple conceptual shift was at work: ideas of 'uncleanness' and 'pollution' in the moral sense became medicalised into physical forms, as infection, degeneration and corruption of the body and mind. The Catholic Church taught that masturbation is worse than rape because at least the latter might result in conception. The same moral premise is at work in the Catholic claim that contraception is bad for health (although, illogically, Catholics do not see celibacy as likewise unhealthy).

Christian moralising is tragically blameable for a vast degree of suffering caused by its absurd attitudes to sex. Leave aside the psychological tortures of frustration, anxiety and guilt, distorted or truncated sexuality, and the harm done by damming the natural outlets of sexual expression, and consider a single example: the treatment of those who fell victim to syphilis when it appeared in Europe in the early sixteenth century.

The 'pox' spread rapidly, afflicting victims with painful and foully suppurating sores that ate away flesh and bone, eroding lips, noses and palates to give sufferers a hideous appearance. Many died at the first onset of the disease in this form; for those who survived, longer-term horrors awaited in the form of bone deformations and insanity before death released them.

The church's response was to say that the disease is God's punishment for lust, and since the sufferers had brought the punishment on themselves they must be shunned. To help its victims was to foil God's purpose in afflicting their bodies to save their souls. To help people avoid the disease with information or protective devices like condoms was to condone and encourage lust. So the church opposed prevention, and when people contracted the disease, it opposed treatment. As it happened, their opposition to treatment was almost a kindness, for what doctors offered sufferers was worse than the disease – cauterisation of their sores with white-hot pokers, steaming in toxic mercury vapour, and trepanning (drilling a hole in the head) to relieve the disease's fearsome headaches.

The response to the AIDS epidemic in contemporary America repeats the medieval response to sex-related disease almost exactly. Leaders of the religious Right call it God's punishment on wickedness, and regard it as self-inflicted. They therefore say that those with AIDS deserve condemnation, not sympathy. In the first two crucial decades of the outbreak, information and measures to prevent its spread were opposed on the grounds that they would promote promiscuity. This recurrence of the same old patterns inevitably produced the same results: moral outrage inhibited and disrupted the search for treatments and the provision of help, thus increasing suffering. To put it in hard practical terms: the religious Right in America is responsible for tens of thousands of AIDS deaths that could have been delayed, or eased, or prevented altogether, because of their influence on the Reagan White House and public support for health measures. This is a dispiriting tale, but although it is not a new one, it reminds us that of all the diseases that afflict humankind, religious moralities are among the worst.

'Sin', remember, means 'disobedience'. If a god ordered you to cut your son's throat (as Yahweh once ordered Abraham) and you refused, you would be a sinner. If you complied, you would count as a good person. Fundamentalists of various kinds murder those whom they see as infidels and apostates, and think of themselves as very good people therefore, because they see what they do as absolute obedience to the will of their deity.

This is the central concept of Islam – the very word means 'submission to God' – but it is a commonplace of fundamentalism in every religion. If the votaries of submission themselves die in the process of obeying their god, they thereby attain the holy status of martyrs, which is why so many seek that end.

Famously, humanity's first sin was quintessential, according to the Book of Genesis, in being an act of disobedience. Adam and Eve ate the fruit of the tree of knowledge in defiance of a divine proscription against doing so, and as a result the whole of mankind has since been punished by work and death. The justice of this arrangement does not seem to have been much questioned in the theological schools, whose energies have gone, instead, into justifying it.

# Repentance

*Our repentance is not so much regret for the evil we have done as fear of what might happen to us because of it.*

LA ROCHEFOUCAULD

In the last year of the twentieth century the Pope publicly repented on behalf of his church for its errors over the preceding two millennia, citing 'betrayal of the Gospel' and 'deviations' from its message. Among other things, he had in mind the Crusades, the Inquisition, holy wars, the torture and burning of heretics, ethnic cleansing and genocide, forced conversions of Indians and Africans, discrimination against women, including their enslavement by excessive childbirth with resulting poverty and ill-health, and the church's role in the Holocaust. Not all of these matters were explicitly mentioned – the Holocaust, for example, was left out – but they were all hinted at, and in explanation of why the list was unspecific a Vatican spokesman said, 'Given the number of sins committed in the course of twenty centuries, it must necessarily be rather summary.'

Repentance means changing one's mind. Students of art history learn how to recognise the *pentamenti* in a painter's work: the alterations, over-paintings, erasures and adjustments detectable most clearly by X-rays, which reveal the painting's evolution and, indirectly therefore, its maker's intentions.

One needs to X-ray the papal apology to understand its evolution. Nearly a decade before he gave the official apology, the Pope reopened the idea of purging the church's conscience, but in its circumspect way the church required that a report first be prepared, to explore the precedents and consequences of such an action, and to assess how far the apology should go – for after all, as the resulting document issued by the International Theological Commission pointed out, many of the sins were committed 'in the service of truth' – as, for example, the massacre of Cathars and the burning of heretics, who were all in danger of getting deeper into the frightful sin of heresy if they were not quickly despatched, for their own good, to Purgatory. (Some definitions: heresy = disagreeing with the church; truth = agreeing with the church.)

The Commission's quest for precedents must have been heartening, for the Pope turns out to be in good company: no less a personage than God is given to repenting, as when in Genesis 6:6 he repents that he had made man, and in 1 Samuel 15 that he had made Samuel king, and even – after being given a stiff lecture by Moses – in Exodus 32:14 that he had been on the point of letting his wrath wax hot against his stiff-necked people. As his various mass murders in the form of punitive floods, earthquakes and immolations attest, however, the deity did not repent often enough; which might explain the church's 2000-year delay in its own first effort.

That God repented at all has been a problem for theologians, for there is an embarrassing contradiction between divine perfections and divine repentings. Apologetical writings on the subject accordingly have chapter headings like 'God repents (1 Sam, 15:35) but this does not mean he was mistaken or in error (Psalm 110:4)'. The Theological Commission ought to have taken this tack in the Papal apology: a form of words which more circumloquaciously said 'We were wrong but we weren't wrong' would have done: given the other things a religion expects people to believe, this claim is a snip.

'Sinning is the best part of repentance,' says an Arab proverb, and one suspects that the church, in the heyday of its power and influence, would have given not a moment's consideration to the idea of repenting *en masse* (and in a mass) for its 'sins of twenty centuries'. In a lecture to Roman Catholics on the Jewish concept of *teshuva*, Rabbi David Blumenthal observed that in addition to acceptance of one's sinfulness and remorse for it, repentance involves restitution. This opens an interesting possibility: will the church, which is very rich, compensate its victims or their heirs now that it has acknowledged its sins against them? Restitution is not a canonical part of Catholic doctrine on repentance, but something Melancthon says suggests it could become so: he describes repentance as consisting of 'contrition, that is, terrors smiting the conscience through the knowledge of sin ... (and) faith ... from which good works, which are the fruits of repentance, are bound to follow.' This, at least, suggests how to test the sincerity of an apology; we wait with bated breath.

Perhaps restitution is essential, on the grounds that apology is not enough. An apology can sometimes help victims, at least in being a recognition of their suffering – and in giving them a modest revenge, for 'he punishes himself who repents of his deeds', as Publilius Syrus said. But it does not repair the damage or reverse the injustices of history. When apologies are offered too late, or only because they have become unavoidable, they are worth little. How  much better it would be if they had not been necessary in the first place.

As Mark Twain points out, we always think of repentance as related to our sins, never as something we feel for our good deeds. But in fact, whereas for the most part we coldly, perfunctorily, and readily repent the bad things we have done, our repentance for good deeds comes 'hot and bitter and straight from the heart' and is rarely forgotten. 'A great benefaction conferred with your whole heart upon an ungrateful man – with what immortal persistence and never-cooling energy do you repent of that!' wrote Twain; 'Repentance of sin is a pale, poor, perishable thing compared with it.' And he continues:

> In my time I have committed several millions of sins. Many of them I probably repented of – I do not remember now; others I was partly minded to repent of, but it did not seem worthwhile; all of them but a few recent ones and a few scattering former ones I have forgotten. In my time I have done eleven good deeds. I remember all of them, four of them with crystal clearness. These four I repent of whenever I think of them – and it is not seldomer than fifty-two times a year. I repent of them in the same old original furious way, undiminished, always. If I wake up away in the night, they are there, waiting and ready; and they keep me company till morning. I have not committed any sin that has lasted me with the unmodifying earnestness and sincerity with which I have repented of these four gracious and beautiful good deeds.

# Faith

*Faith, like a jackal, feeds among the tombs, and even from these dead doubts she gathers her most vital hope.*

HERMAN MELVILLE

Some religious devotees feel so embattled and embittered by the questioning or rejection of their cherished beliefs that they are prepared to resort to murder, even indiscriminate mass murder, as happens wherever fanaticism mixes with resentment and ignorance to produce the hateful brew of what is done in the name of belief. 'Faith is what I die for, dogma is what I kill for,' as the saying has it; and the trouble is that all faith is based on dogma.

It is a curious fact that responsible enquiry, of the kind conducted by scientists and expected in courts of law, is careful in drawing its conclusions, and open-minded about the possibility of contrary future evidence, whereas, in sharp contrast, matters of faith are tenaciously regarded as inviolable, irrefutable, and unrevisable. The careful and open-minded procedures of science have given us electric light, antibiotics, central heating, television and computers. Science has often been perverted to bad uses – bombs and gas-chambers – but it is politics and politicians, not science and scientists, who do that. Religious belief, meanwhile, whatever it might do in comforting the fearful in the dark, has always and everywhere brought war, intolerance and persecution with it, and has distorted human nature into false and artificial shapes. Some try to palliate or even excuse the crimes committed by religion in human history by invoking the glorious art and music it has produced; to which the answer is that Greek mythology and secular avocations have done the same, without burning anyone at the stake in the process.

Faith is a negation of reason. Reason is the faculty of pro-portioning judgment to evidence, after first weighing the evidence. Faith is belief even in the face of contrary evidence. Søren Kierkegaard defined faith as the leap taken despite everything, despite the very absurdity of what one is asked to believe. When people can doggedly choose to believe that black is white, and can, in their utter certainty, go so far as to shoot you because you do not agree, there is little room for debate. 'Faith, fanatic Faith, once wedded fast to some dear falsehood, hugs it to the last,' says Thomas Moore's 'Veiled Prophet of Khorassan'.

In the branch of philosophy called 'epistemology' – the theory of knowledge – knowledge is defined as belief which is both true and justified. One main theory describes knowledge as a rela-tionship between a state of mind and a fact. The content of the mental state is a judgment responsibly made, and the fact is (for example) some arrangement of the world which, when the judg-ment is true, is what makes it so. Belief differs from knowledge in that whereas the latter is controlled by the facts, and depends upon the right kind of relationship between mind and world, the former is all and only in the mind, and does not rely on anything in the world. One can, in short, believe anything: that pigs fly, that grass is blue, and that people who do not believe either are wicked. This is what makes St Augustine's remark that 'faith is to believe what you do not see; the reward for faith is to see what you believe', so sinister; for if one can believe anything, one can 'see' anything – and therefore feel entitled to do anything accordingly: to live like an Old Testament patriarch, which is silly, or even to kill another human being, which is vile.

*

It must strike even desultory readers of the Old Testament that the god it depicts – a tribal deity – is a bully and a tyrant of the first water. The contrast with the New Testament's avuncular deity is striking. But what readers might not know is that some biblical texts have a decidedly questionable history. Consider Deuteronomy, which in the midst of yet another doctrinal quarrel within Israel, was suddenly and conveniently 'found' by workmen refurbishing the Temple; and of course it gave unequivocal support to one side of the argument. Yahweh often entered on cue like this, apparently unable to resist politics; and invariably on the winning side.

Jesus's divinity affords another example. In Mark's Gospel he is a man; in the theology of St Paul he is the medium of the New Covenant; in the fourth century AD, after a massive controversy over the Arian 'heresy' – Arius of Alexandria had argued that Jesus must be less divine than the Father – he became a god in human form.

An intriguing argument is offered by Karen Armstrong concerning the rise of Islam, which, she claims, resulted from an Arabic sense of inferiority. Arabs, she says, felt 'mingled resentment and respect' for Jews and Christians because they had enjoyed direct communication with God. Leaders like Zayd ibn Amr longed for their own people to receive a divine revelation. It came at last to Muhammad ibn Abdallah in a terrifying experience on Mount Hira outside Mecca, in which the angel Gabriel instructed him to 'Recite!' The result, produced at laborious intervals over the following two decades, was the Koran, the 'Recitation', whose sheer beauty of language is reputed to have been a frequent instrument of conversion in its own right.

But as with Christianity, splits and controversies followed, and Islam's early tolerance towards other religions soon vanished, as did the early freedoms enjoyed by its women. And again as with Christianity, the long-term legacy includes the familiar horrors of intolerance, bigotry and persecution which characterise all organised religion.

The concept of God, as these thoughts show, is a gerrymandered affair. It is an invention of man, because humans are spiritual creatures, and spirituality matters. Some of us argue that only art and affection can appease its hungers. Rather than seek new definitions of deity, or 'New Age' religions, we do better to dispense with theologies altogether, and place our hopes in the best of things human instead.

If one wished for a particular illustration of why, no better example could be adduced than that of Urbain Grandier, a man who made a fatal mistake long ago, in the year 1618. Grandier's wit, his intelligence, his worldly ways, the romantic scandals in which he became embroiled, would not by themselves have ensured his downfall, even though he was a politically active priest in a region of France where relations between the Catholic Church and the Huguenots were tense. But his wit was of the satirical kind, and when in that year he ridiculed a government minister called Armand Jean du Plessis, he did not know how high his enemy would eventually rise, nor how unforgiving his enemy's powers of memory would prove; for Armand was the future Cardinal Richelieu.

Twelve years later Grandier was accused by the nuns of the Ursuline convent in Loudun, where he was priest of St-Pierre-du-Marche, of conjuring demons into them. The nuns knew that Grandier, tall and handsome, and a spell-binding orator, counted among his notorious liaisons a love affair with Madeleine de Brou, to whom he dedicated a treatise on why it is theologically permissible for priests to marry. Bewitched by him psychologically, the nuns came to think they had been bewitched by him literally. Following a visitation of the plague in 1630 there was a series of hysterical outbreaks in the convent, which began to coalesce around references to Grandier, and finally into accusations that he had summoned the devil to possess not only the Mother Superior, Jeanne des Anges, but most of the other nuns. The result is well known, in film and story, as the 'Possession of Loudun'.

There was an inquiry after the first outbreak among the nuns, but local scepticism and the more influential disbelief of the Bishop of Poitiers and the Archbishop of Bordeaux put an end to it. Not long afterwards, pursuing a general policy of demilitarising France's provinces, Richelieu sent his agent Laubardemont to Loudun to supervise the demolition of its fortifications. This policy was unpopular in Loudun as elsewhere, for in depriving provincial towns of their defences it exposed them to the depredations of mercenary armies. Demolition of the walls was therefore resisted, and in Loudun one of the leaders of the opposition was Urbain Grandier. Laubardemont reported back to Richelieu, who instantly saw his chance to remove an impediment and settle an old score simultaneously. He instructed Laubardemont to reopen the demonism enquiry, and a terrible inexorability entered the picture.

Three exorcists – a Capuchin, a Franciscan and a Jesuit – set to work on the nuns of Loudun, interrogating the devils in Latin and Hebrew. Such writhings of bodies followed, and such lewd displays and language by the contorted women of the Ursuline convent, that all France was set alight. The demons were ordered to reveal who had summoned them into the nuns' bodies, and with one voice they replied 'Urbain Grandier!' The proceedings were public; up to 7000 people at a time witnessed the devil-prompted indecencies committed by the nuns. The Jesuit exorcist himself became possessed by devils, and Jeanne des Anges, when she had recovered from her ordeal, became a national celebrity, travelling all over France to speak of her adventures.

The principal evidence against Urbain Grandier was a contract he had signed with Satan and assorted subordinate devils, all of whom – Astoroth, Beelzebub, and Leviathan among them –

had put their signatures to the document too, in flourishing calligraphy. On such conclusive evidence Grandier's case was hopeless. Before being burned alive at the stake (lesser felons were strangled before the flames were lit) he was tortured in the 'boots', a contraption designed to crush the prisoner's feet and lower limbs. His exorcists, fearing that the common executioner would not be strong enough to overcome the resistance of the devils in Grandier, wielded the hammers themselves. He was dragged from the torture chamber to the stake, and even as (according to one witness) the blood and marrow from his mangled legs left a trail on the cobblestones, some of the nuns took pity on him and tried to recant. To the exorcists this was proof that the devils were not quite yet banished.

To read about the terrible fate of Urbain Grandier is to follow – step by inexorable step – a black story of intrigue, politics, malice, duplicity, credulity, suffering and madness. Alas, it is not unusual in the history either of human folly or the crimes of religion.

Grandier's fate is the fate of a man lost under the joint government of religious superstition and human malice – a natural and ancient partnership. Malice will always be with us, one supposes, but a question can be asked about the other half of the equation. Does religious superstition any longer deserve a place in the intellectual economy of the world?

The history of human knowledge shows that it does not. Religion is the legacy of our cave-men ancestors. Religious beliefs constituted their science, religious practices their higher technology. As the former it offered them explanations of wind and storm, the origin of the world, the meaning of the stars. As the latter it offered a means of avoiding drought, curing illness, and winning wars – by prayer, sacrifice, and the careful observance of taboos and rituals, all aimed at pleasing or at least appeasing the mysterious and often terrible forces which seemed to them to govern the world.

God, accordingly, is the name of our ignorance. As real knowledge and mastery advance, there is diminishing need to invoke supernatural agencies to explain the world. Deities inhabit the dark places over the horizon of knowledge, and retreat as light approaches. Yet the priests of these ancient ignorances, claiming their authority, exhort us to restrict our behaviour in a variety of ways, some of the restrictions being merely odd (avoid meat on Fridays) and some demonstrably harmful to our well-being (frustrate your natural affections).

Perhaps the most striking conflict between ancient ignorance and modern knowledge is found in the competing accounts they offer of the origin and nature of the universe. Each of the world's many religions has its own version of a tale in which some or other supernatural agency acts upon chaos to bring the world into being, the task taking anything between an instant and a week. Few of them offer any account of the agency's origins, which are left in mystery. For most religions the creation story is a fact of faith, an absolute truth. Contemporary science hypothesises an evolutionary tale of physical forces. I say 'hypothesises', note; hypothesises on the basis of good evidence, severely tested, with many aspects of the accompanying theory successfully applied to daily life – as exemplified by the light you read by, the computer you work on, the airplane you fly in. The great advantage of science's careful and thorough hypotheses, always ready to yield if better evidence comes along, is that it makes use of no materials or speculations beyond what the world itself offers. Religions, in sharp contrast, offer us eternal certitudes on the basis only of ancient superstitions.

Some scientists, amazingly, are religious, and they are apt to say that the best argument they can give for having religious beliefs is the so-called 'argument to the best explanation', which in this case says that, given the inconclusiveness of our state of knowledge, the best account we can give of the world is that there is a God.

This argument is famously weak. Two thoughts show why. One is that it is very far from clear that theism is the best explanation for the existence and nature of the world, especially as by citing the existence and activity of a deity to answer questions about why there is a world and how it came into being, it simply shifts the problem back a step – to questions about why there is a deity, and how *it* came into being. Secondly, there is the simple fact that even if, improbably, appeal to the existence of a deity were the best explanation human intelligence could invent, the fact is that what looks like the best explanation in any subject matter can be wrong. Such arguments are intrinsically feeble; they amount to saying, 'This is the best we can do to explain such-and-such in our present state of ignorance.' And ignorance is the key: gods invariably inhabit the shadowy realm of ignorance beyond the horizon of knowledge, a horizon which recedes before us – taking its supernatural baggage as it goes – as enquiry advances.

Science, one would think, has put the ancient superstitions to flight. A mighty battle was fought in the nineteenth century over this matter in respect of Christianity; its history is a complicated one, but religious missions – not just to Africa and the Far East but to the slums of London and New York, in all cases proselytising the ignorant and unlettered who had not heard of science – saved the churches and laid the basis for the many fundamentalist denominations prevalent in the world today among peoples once colonised by the European powers.

Religious apologists speak much about beauty and goodness, personhood, and subjective experience. These are indeed the things that matter most. But apologists make the standard mistake – and often wilfully make it – of conflating these high and good matters of human experience with anything supernatural. Humanity's sense of beauty, and decency, our power to love, our creativity – all the best things about us – belong to us, to human experience in the real world. They neither need, nor benefit from, some alleged connection with supernatural agencies of one kind or another. They are ours, just as much as the evil, stupidity, greed and cruelty which they oppose. Indeed: why do not religious apologists say that these bad things come from the gods, the better things from man, rather than – as they always claim – the other way round?

# Miracles

*Men talk about Bible miracles because there is no miracle in their lives. Cease to gnaw that crust. There is ripe fruit over your head.*

THOREAU

The happy fact about miracles is that they require no support in the way of evidence or rational evaluation. Indeed, they do better without them. Mark Twain illustrates this by relating how an enquirer asked a celebrated professor whether recently-received reports (it was then 1909) claiming that Dr Frederick Cook had discovered the North Pole were true. 'The answer, yes or no,' replied the professor, 'depends entirely upon the answer to this question: Is it claimed that Dr Cook's achievement is a Fact, or a Miracle? If it is a Miracle, any sort of evidence will answer, but if it is a Fact, proof is necessary.' 'Is that the law?' asked the enquirer. 'Yes,' said the professor, 'it is absolute. Modifications of it are not permissible. A very pertinent remark has been quoted from the Westminster Gazette, which points out that "the golfer, when he puts in a record round, has to have his card signed, and that there is nobody to sign Dr Cook's card; there are two Eskimos to vouch for his feat, to be sure, but they were his caddies, and at golf their evidence would not be accepted." There you have the whole case. If Dr Cook's feat is put forward as Fact, the evidence of the two caddies is inadequate; if it is put forward as Miracle, one caddy is plenty.'

Miracles are standardly described as supernatural abrogations of the laws of nature. Some believers hold that they are not abrogations of nature's laws, but only seem that way to ignorant humanity. In any event they are extremely non-standard events. Obviously, the concept of the miraculous is very useful because it can be invoked to explain anything whatever. But therein also lies its weakness; as David Hume pointed out, when one weighs the evidence supporting the regular functioning of natural laws with evidence supporting claims that there has been a singular violation of them, the former must always so far outweigh the latter as to render them nugatory. And he added that it is infinitely more likely that a person who claims to have witnessed a miracle is mistaken, or deluded, or lying, than that the relevant laws of nature should in fact have been abolished temporarily for some local purpose.

There is another and better sense of 'miracle', a colloquial one, denoting what is wonderful in both nature and human nature at their best. No gods are needed to explain them, and the only faith required is in the world's own capacity for good – a capacity which, in its variety and extent, is itself miraculous.

# Prophecy

*Study prophecies when they are become histories.*

SIR THOMAS BROWNE

It seems that the third prophecy of Fatima, kept secret until recently, concerned the assassination attempt on the Pope in 1981. Heaven's choice of what to alert us to is a mystery – the famines, genocides, earthquakes and plagues provided by the divine mercy since Fatima were not advertised as forthcoming in its bulletin, yet the assassination attempt was. According to a Cardinal who is the Vatican secretary of state, a complete text of the prophecy will be published after what he unblushingly describes as 'appropriate' preparation, so perhaps the special significance of the event will be explained.

Still, the banality of most Christian messages from heaven since St John (the Apocalypse is a hard act to follow) is something of a relief in comparison to those in other religions, which seem mainly to encourage the murder of heretics (i.e. those who disagree with the leaders of the faith in question).

News that the third prophecy of Fatima was fulfilled two decades ago suggests that the Vatican know Thomas Browne's remark, quoted above. Prophecies are always more plausible when their futures are in our pasts, so that we can interpret them historically. As with Rorschach blots, the past is very generous in the interpretations it admits. If, as with the quatrains of Nostradamus, the prophecies themselves are couched in maximally obscure terms, a happy marriage results: all prophecies can be made to come out true.

In biblical times, and for a long period afterwards, 'prophecy' meant interpreting the will of God. A prophet was a teacher, a moralist, as well as a forecaster. All religions and traditions have their seers. Apollo, frustrated in his passion for the chaste Cassandra, cursed her prophecies so that no one would believe them. Tiresias the blind seer saw more and further than any sighted man. Soothsayers have never been short of work because humans are superstitious and life is uncertain – a profitable combination from the soothsayer's point of view. The church condemned many seers as votaries of Satan, on the grounds that attempting to know the future is sinful. This applied only to prophecy not licensed by the church itself, of course, and represents a market strategy for undermining the competition.

Prophecy in the sense of foretelling the future makes sense only if determinism is true – that is, if the future history of the world is already settled and fixed. Theologians have their work cut out reconciling the free will required for sin with the omniscience of God who, knowing everything, knows what is to come. The medieval Schoolmen devised elaborate explanations of how human freedom and divine foreknowledge can coexist. For sheer ingenuity their arguments earn high marks.

Prophecy has a respectable and necessary cousin, which is rational forecasting based on past experience and current data, with a view to assessing what is more probable than not in such matters as tomorrow's weather, next year's social trends, and the long-term effects of cigarette-smoking and pollution. All life is movement into the future, and therefore planning and preparing is essential if life is to be worth living. The premise of this view is the exact opposite of the one underlying belief in prophecy: it is that the future does not yet exist, but is ours to make – and that we can make it best on the basis of intelligent understanding of the past and present.

Even in antiquity the examination of auspices was not always seen as predictive, but as revealing the current state of the gods' attitudes. If the gods were hostile, the likelihood was that the proposed venture – a battle, or the building of a palace – would fail. But enough libations and sacrifices could change the gods' minds, securing success. Some ancient philosophers recognised the startling implication of this idea. It is that if we can influence what will happen, we are therefore responsible for what will happen, for even doing nothing is a choice. Regarding the future as open therefore makes us the captains of our fate. To think the opposite – that prophecy is possible, and that therefore the future is fixed – leaves us merely fate's victims.

# Virginity

*Too chaste an adolescence makes for a dissolute old age.*

ANDRÉ GIDE

There is a general social consensus against teenage pregnancy, for familiar reasons; and one part of the effort at encouraging young women to avoid it is to encourage them to be chaste – or to use a term preferred by tabloid editors, to remain virgins. The modern assumption that motherhood should be postponed to the third decade of a woman's life reflects changed views about how much educational preparation is needed for our complex society – and about the nature of youth, now seen as a holiday season spoiled by too much early responsibility.

These views present an interesting contrast with the fact that most mothers in the world's history began their maternal careers as teenagers, biologically an excellent time for it. In many places they still do. In parallel, teenage boys began apprenticeships or other forms of work then too. Youth was a luxury that poverty could not afford, and parenthood was an economic necessity, providing more hands for the plough and insurance for the parents' old age. Now, in the wealthy West, youth is seen as an amenity – mainly by those who have lost it.

Tabloid editors would not treat virginity as a titillating topic if it had not long ago been invested with moral significance by various religious traditions, who provided strong support to the idea that women should be virgins when they marry so that men of substance could be certain they were going to be the fathers of the children destined to inherit their property. Virginity until marriage has been a necessity for women in many dispensations, its absence incurring harsh punishments – the death penalty, or at least shame and ostracism. In some traditions today the barbaric act of infibulating girls – stitching them closed – as a way of ensuring virginity still continues.

If the practical reason for enjoining female virginity was once inheritance, the metaphysical reason was that the soul, akin to air and heaven, is pure, but the body, akin to earth and passion, is impure; thus sexuality is dirty, chastity clean. St Paul's dislike of women prompted him to discourage sex, and the Neoplatonists, three centuries later, imported a full-blooded theory of spiritual purity and bodily uncleanness into Christianity, finishing what St Paul started. The rest is – unhappy – history.

But Christianity was not alone. Rome's Vestal Virgins were put to death if they lost their virginity, such was their importance in tending the sacred flame in the Temple of Vesta. The manner of execution was live burial. They were six in all, selected from patrician families before the age of ten and committed to thirty years of virginity thereafter. If challenged they had to prove their virginity by carrying water in a sieve from the River Tiber – easy to do if they remembered to grease the sieve first (and they knew enough colloid chemistry to do it).

They also knew that virginity and chastity are not the same thing; a woman could technically be a virgin while enjoying a happy and flourishing sex life in other ways. The Christian ideal of marriage likewise recognised that a woman might be married and therefore not a virgin, but that she could still be chaste, in the sense that although she had relations with her husband she need not enjoy them – indeed, said the priests, unclean thoughts or feelings during sex were deemed likely to cause deformities in a child then conceived.

As this shows, what underlies talk of virginity is a profound and often hidden moral *angst* about purity and pollution – and therefore also sentiments of temptation and desire. If our religions had decided that ears or wisdom teeth were spiritually significant, we should feel the same anxieties regarding them as with the hymen; and moral concern would be devoted to them instead.

# Paganism

Men become superstitious not because they have too much imagination, but because they are not aware that they have any.

SANTAYANA

Many of the feasts of the Christian calendar began as pagan festivals, and were adopted and adapted by the church as a means of winning converts. Easter, for example, has its origins in a pagan celebration of nature's resurrection. According to St Bede, the word is derived from Scandinavian *Ostra* or Teutonic *Ostern* or *Eastre*, in either case the name of a goddess of northern mythology responsible for fertility and birth – although scholars now disagree with him (and among themselves) about these etymologies. The symbols of Easter, rabbits and eggs, are as ancient as the festival: rabbits signify reproductive ebullience, eggs symbolise new life. Like the phallus-worshipping May-day observance which closely follows it (and which contemporary self-styled 'Pagans' regard as a more important feast, a 'Greater Sabbat' as opposed to a 'Lesser Sabbat'), Easter is therefore about sex. The contrast with the purely spiritual and other-worldly significance now attached to it is striking proof that propaganda and brutality (e.g. burnings at the stake) can make entire populations believe the very opposite of what their ancestors believed.

Christianity's appropriation of this age-old fertility festival is of a piece with its frequent adaptation of other once-pagan things. The quarter-days, including Christmas, are associated with moments of astronomical importance, namely the solstices of winter and summer and the equinoxes of spring and autumn, all of them major pagan feasts. Many of the saints of the Christian calendar are pagan deities whose cult was so strong that the new religion could make headway only by incorporating them; two of many examples are St Vitus and St Hippolytus. Fraser in *The Golden Bough* famously begins by showing how worship of the Virgin Mary was grafted onto worship of the virgin goddess Diana, whose cult in Italy during the first centuries AD was very powerful. The Christians' technique was effective; the old faiths were simply incorporated wholesale into the new; Diana's worshippers were told that they could at last know her real name, which was Mary.

Indeed, the very word 'pagan' with its negative connotations, is a mark of Christianity's propaganda success. In Latin *paganus* means 'countryman', and by association 'pagan' even then denoted the superstitions of uneducated folk. Worship of nature and its animating principles, together with knowledge of nature's healing and narcotic powers, and celebration of everything associated with its cycles of reproduction, birth, maturation and death, were outlawed by Christians as evil practices. The beings associated with these superstitions – the Green Man, the nature goddesses, fairies and elves – were demonised. Nature, like the human body itself, was to be chastened and controlled, as merely functional and not only far less significant than the abstract spiritual truths of the next world, but actively hostile to them unless subjugated.

The nature beliefs characteristic of ancient paganism (and modern 'Paganism') reflect the origins of religion as mankind's first attempt at science and technology. It was science because it offered an account of how the world works; it taught that the wind blows because invisible powers puff their cheeks and blow, and likewise that crops grow and rains fall at the will – or when otherwise, the whim – of the gods. It was therefore technology also because it offered a means of controlling the wind, rain and growth of crops, the means being prayer and sacrifice.

There was nothing arbitrary about these beliefs for our ancestors. They could see the gods in the sky – the sun and moon – and feel their strength in the earthquake and their anger in the drought. It is a mark of how entrenched that world-view remains that as its themes became increasingly abstract, belief in them appears to have grown stronger. Thus: the ancient Egyptians married a boy to their queen on the day of the winter solstice, then at the day's end killed and dismembered him to strew his body on the fields like fertiliser, the point being to encourage the sun to cease its southward winter journey and brings it life-giving warmth back again so that the crops would grow. This theme – of death being a necessary preliminary to renewed life – is repeated in many traditions; it has echoes in the tale of Orpheus's journey to and from the underworld, and it makes Jesus's three days in hell a commonplace of mythology.

In Western Christianity Easter is the first Sunday after the full moon that follows the spring equinox of 21 March. This is why it is a 'movable feast'. In Eastern Christianity it coincides with the Jewish observance of Passover, for the reason that the earliest Christians, who were Jews, appropriated the latter for their new rites. Every Easter votaries of both traditions now repeat the paradox that is so characteristic of human beings: they watch Easter services on television, thereby using an instrument of science to replenish their faith in dim superstitions whose roots lie in the infancy of our species, and which were dreamed up then to fill the vacuum of humanity's early ignorance.

# Blasphemy

*All great truths begin as blasphemies.*

GEORGE BERNARD SHAW

If I impugn your God or gods, in your view I blaspheme. So if an alien comes to a Christian country and tells its devout citizens that their belief in virgin birth, miracles, resurrection, and so forth, is nonsense, and that they should instead bow down before the horned toad as the true incarnation of deity, that alien would be branded a blasphemer. The alien, of course, would retort the charge on his accusers' heads. And so it would go on, until either he or they were reduced to cinders at some convenient stake.

It is hard to give a straightforward definition of blasphemy, because blasphemy comes into existence when something that someone says or writes gives a special kind of offence to someone else, the offence typically consisting in a perceived insult to something cherished as divine. But it depends on cases; and it always takes two – a giver and a receiver of offence – to make blasphemy possible. We gain insights into the concept by looking at examples of its application. Consider the story of the Italian miller Menocchio, brilliantly told in Carlo Ginzburg's classic *The Cheese and the Worms*. Menocchio perished at the stake in 1600 for denying the virginity of Mary and the divinity of Jesus. He had his own theology, which he attempted to persuade his contemporaries to accept; but because it was not the theology of the Inquisition, he died at the stake. Examples can be multiplied endlessly; what they have in common is: difference in perception, with the stronger power persecuting the weaker as a result.

It is a mistake to think that controversies over blasphemy are, despite occasional flare-ups like the Rushdie affair, dying out. It is a Freudian idea that religion, like perversion, is a precultural phenomenon, belonging to the infancy of mankind, and that with its slow demise go all the appurtenances of belief in witchcraft, evil, devil-possession, heresy, blasphemy and the like. But although Freud all his life opposed religion as a sinister force that must be defeated – he was a 'master blasphemer' in this sense – the threat of conflict always lurks. Blasphemy is a destructive idea, a dangerous, subjective catch-all used by superstitious people to deny others their liberty of thought. The world would be a better place if the notion were purged from it.

And that in particular means that blasphemy laws should be abolished wherever they still exist. Such laws, like those about obscenity and censorship, are simply instruments for controlling ideas. Thus viewed, blasphemy is a healthy phenomenon because it is a sign of free speech, and demonstrates the maturing of society from one level of belief and practice to another.

# Obscenity

*'Obscenity' is not a term capable of exact legal definition; in the practice of the Courts, it means 'anything that shocks the magistrate'.*

BERTRAND RUSSELL

In 1857, as the Victorian era was beginning its surge towards its high point, the British Parliament passed an act to control 'obscene literature'. This was the Obscene Publications Act of 1857, and it was the result of persistent and well-organised lobbying by anti-vice church groups.

The measure was introduced to Parliament by the then Lord Chief Justice, Lord Campbell, with the express purpose of furnishing magistrates with powers to seize and destroy sexually explicit literature. In the event the Act came to be worded in a way more restricted than Campbell wished, giving magistrates powers to control literature which existed 'for the single purpose of corrupting the morals of youth and of a nature calculated to shock the common feelings of decency in any well regulated mind.' This restriction was imposed on Campbell's Bill by a sceptical Parliament which, even at this point in the evolution of the Victorian period, was wary of censorship.

But the narrow focus of the Act's intentions was almost immediately ignored in judicial interpretations. In 1868 Campbell's successor, Lord Cockburn, ruled that the test of obscenity implied by the Act was 'whether the tendency of the matter charged as obscene is to deprave and corrupt those whose

minds are open to such immoral influences.' On this interpretation the Act proceeded to do untold damage to the literature of Britain, and its effects are still being felt.

Among the Act's early victims were Charles Bradlaugh and
Annie Besant for publishing a pamphlet on birth control. They
were sentenced to six months in prison apiece, and their sen-
tences were overturned on appeal only on a technicality. In a
more celebrated case, Henry Vizetelly spent three months in
prison in 1889 for publishing the first English translation of
Zola's *La Terre* (The Soil). Not only fiction but science was
affected; the first volume of Havelock Ellis's *Study in the Psychology of Sex* was also prosecuted.

Thus was the scene set for a war of attrition on English
letters in the twentieth century, a saga equally absorbing and
dismaying. Stanley Baldwin's Home Secretary, William
Joynson-Hicks ('Jix'), was a crusading moralist whose determination to ban Joyce's *Ulysses* and Radclyffe Hall's *The Well
of Loneliness* in the 1920s marks an especially low point in the
puritanical hatred – or is it fear? perhaps there was no difference – of sex in British society. The *Ulysses* ban was in effect
based on a reading by the Director of Public Prosecutions of
only forty of the book's seven hundred pages, and was as much
motivated by suspicion of Joyce himself – an Irishman, after
all – as disgust over Molly's masturbatory meditations.

Another outburst of puritanism occurred in the 1950s, largely
aimed at damming the flood of cheap pulp fiction from America.
But it even took in the saucy seaside postcard, one of whose
principal producers, Donald McGill, found himself in court. A
'Blue Book' of suspect publications was circulated to Chief
Constables by the Home Office; its existence was kept secret
not just from the public but also from MPs. It contained 4000
titles, including books by Mickey Spillane and James Hadley
Chase, Sartre, and Upton Sinclair, and – amazingly – it also listed
*Moll Flanders* and *Madame Bovary*. Into this absurd situation

stepped a knight of sanity: Mr Justice Stable, who presided over an obscenity trial in 1957 involving a book called *The Philanderer*. He told the jury that he thought the Victorians' test of obscenity was no longer good enough; times had changed, and the fact that a book might be unsuitable for adolescents was not a reason to forbid its general sale. He told the jury to read the book as a whole, not concentrating on a few bits here and there. The jury did so, and acquitted the publishers.

At about the same time magistrates in Swindon were making themselves a national laughing-stock by banning Boccaccio's *Decameron* while permitting the sale of Hank Jansen's *Don't Mourn Me Toots*. The combination of events showed that times had already changed. The man who was to prove Britain's best twentieth-century Home Secretary by far, Roy Jenkins, produced from opposition the 1959 Obscene Publications Act, which provided a new defence of obscenity as being for the public good if it serves the interests of science, literature, art or learning. Although in other respects imperfect, the Act by this means has since been a bastion of protection for literature, despite sporadic efforts (by Mary Whitehouse and her like) to keep censorship alive. The Jenkins Act provided the background for enthralling landmark trials which followed, chief among them that of *Lady Chatterley's Lover*, which secured the Act in operation.

But censorship still exists. A brilliant report prepared for the British Government in the 1970s under the chairmanship of the philosopher Bernard Williams, but never acted upon, proposed that all existing obscenity laws should be replaced by a single, comprehensive statute based on a test of 'significant and substantial harm', thus dispensing with the undefined, vague and too widely interpretable current concepts of 'indecency', 'depravity' and 'obscenity'. The Williams proposal serves the cause of free expression against censorship, but does it wisely:

for liberty is not licence, it is something better: it is open-minded, tolerant and reasonable restraint. Only good laws well framed can promote such a thing.

# Poverty

*Poor men's reasons are not heard.*

THOMAS FULLER

One of the measures of a good society is how it treats the poor. It is not always easy for those who are not poor to know how to do this well. 'Short of genius,' observed Charles Péguy, 'a rich man cannot imagine poverty.' That is why the better-off think that poor people should go without television and cigarettes if they cannot afford them. This is a mistake, as an understanding of the nature of poverty shows.

There are several kinds of poverty. Third- and first-world poverty are entirely different in character because of the great difference in their historical and economic settings. The gruel-ling problems faced by the third world's poor relate to bare survival, to the basic task of getting water and food. Their plight is often further complicated by war, corruption, flood or drought. Third-world poverty is life on the margins of existence, a tough and unforgiving struggle, dedicated to the present moment and having room in it for only two feelings: despair and hope.

First-world poverty is a relative matter, but no less painful for being so. Seneca's remark that 'the poor man is not one who has little, but one who hankers after more' applies here. In developed societies possession of the amenities of life – which includes not just objects like houses and motorcars, but also powers, like being able to go out to the cinema or a restaurant, and to take holidays abroad – is equivalent to status, to full membership of the community, to having a place and a voice. Without these things one is less than half a citizen, disempowered and sidelined. It is not merely a matter of symbols. The person who cannot afford a television or newspaper is not only barred from the life of the community, but is even detached from knowing what is happening in it.

Poverty is not a virus, a natural disaster, or an accident. It is man-made. The world's wealth is distributed in a grossly uneven way, not always or often reflecting true value – the managing director of a City company annually earns more than fifty nurses together do, which is a strange fact. 'The rich cannot eat money,' dryly observes a Russian proverb, 'so it's just as well that there are poor folk to grow their food.'

The moral reasons for alleviating the hardships of poverty speak for themselves, but doubtlessly the pragmatic reasons for doing so are more likely to persuade the better-off. In his Yorktown Oration, Robert Winthrop wisely remarked that the poor should be treated liberally 'so that mendicity shall not be tempted into mendacity, nor want exasperated into crime'. The link between poverty on the one hand, and on the other hand social unease, resentment, crime, unrest and eventually upheaval, is obvious enough; but it is not the mere fact of deprivation – by itself rather a damper than an igniter of action – but the sense of exclusion and injustice that grows from it, which drives people to antisocial action.

Few consciously choose poverty – saints and philosophers might, but it does not take one of the latter to teach us that elective poverty is not poverty – and the arrantly feckless and lazy are only a few of that few. 'The rich man may never get into heaven,' remarked Alexander Chase, 'but the poor are already serving their term in hell.'

# Capitalism

*The trouble with the profit system has always been that it is highly unprofitable to most people.*

E. B. WHITE

Few people would claim, at least openly, that they do not wish all societies to be fair and decent. It is of course easier to say that societies should be so than to make them so, especially in an age of globalised free-market capitalism which delivers the good life to most residents of advanced industrial countries – countries which therefore are also the centres of world power and influence, making it no surprise that the virtues of their economic way of life should seem unquestionably superior to alternatives. In the rich West it is now orthodox to think that the ideology of the free market has won the argument – and so comprehensively that the future, like the present, belongs to it; hence Francis Fukuyama's claim that 'history has ended'. Dissenting voices, however eloquent and well informed, are barely audible against the resounding self-confidence of this view. But the story told by dissenting voices is deeply troubling, and makes a powerful case for greater justice and sustainability in the world economy.

Capitalism needs continuing growth in production and therefore consumption to sustain itself. The benefits that have accrued in the way of technology and improved standards of living are obvious and palpable in the rich West. But, say the dissenters, the cost is proving too great, especially in damage to the environment, crippling third-world debt, untenable disparities between rich and poor, and the destructive effect upon communities of turning people into commodities and social relations into market transactions. Dissenters can relentlessly and to disturbing effect quote figures on environmental damage, poverty, waste and third-world exploitation. Facts about the horrendous loss of rain forest acreage each year, about South Asian children stitching together, for a few pence a day, the footballs our own children play with, about famines caused in third-world countries because subsistence agriculture has been replaced by export crops, are all too familiar. Less familiar are such facts as that Mexico's richest man has more money than the poorest seventeen million of his countrymen put together, and that the annual debt repayments of many poor countries far exceed what they can spend on health and education. Such considerations forcibly bring home the injustice and instability of the world economic order, and oblige us to ask not whether but how it should be changed.

Defenders of globalised market capitalism put their faith in two things: the capacity of markets themselves to remedy, in the long run, the worst iniquities and inequities they cause, and the 'technical fix' by which future technological innovation will solve problems created by current technology and industry. For example: future cars, lightbulbs and heating systems will be so clever and efficient, say optimists, that we will consume less energy than now, so it does not matter that we are currently expending our fuel resources at what seems like an unsustainable rate.

Critics are unimpressed by these arguments. They point out that the market exists so that those who control resources can reap profits, which is their single goal and *raison d'être*. In leaving the world prey to impersonal forces of supply and demand, the market ignores the effect on the many who merely serve its interests without sharing its rewards. To achieve social justice, they say, we need an economics that puts human interests at the centre. Such an economics would embody principles affirming environmental and cultural protection, economic justice for individuals and peoples, and regulation of the activities of multinational corporations.

Many theories of sustainable, and therefore more restrained and balanced, economic activity have been offered, but none are likely to be adopted while the current order reaps such rewards for some and holds out such attractions for many. Any change sufficient to reverse the runaway trends of the contemporary order would require massive changes in attitudes and practices, so it is hard to see how it would happen unless some global catastrophe forced it on us.

Some argue that a return to small self-governing communities offers the only hope for a juster and more sustainable future. They have in mind the local, self-sustaining 'peasant culture' which has existed from earliest times, a social arrangement described by one historian as 'humankind's finest achievement'. But this reveals the fatal weakness in all such arguments: as a response to the genuine concerns that the worst aspects of free-market capitalism prompt, recommending a return to peasant life, or indeed to any dispensation of reduced consumption, limited growth, stasis and constraint, is scarcely a serious option, not only for those relatively few who benefit from capitalism, but for those very many who aspire to join them.

Critics of the present world economy are liable to be tendentious in their criticisms, because there truly is much to deplore in its effects on the natural and social world and its rank injustice. They are right to say that something must be done. But as such unsatisfactory proposals illustrate, a convincing way out of the dilemma has yet to be offered.

There are those, however, who not only defend but extol the free-market order and the consumerism which fuels it. Sociological orthodoxy says that consumerism is oppression; skilful marketing people have manipulated us, says this orthodoxy, into a state of passive victimhood, endlessly and aimlessly consuming ever-increasing amounts at the behest of an advertising industry which creates false desires in us by making us believe that to purchase an object is to purchase happiness. Studies of consumerism and what it involves – marketing, brand names, fashion, shopping, packaging, rubbish, pollution, social rivalry, the throw-away ethos and the commodification of value – make disturbing reading, because they suggest that the mechanisms of persuasion and coercion underlying capitalism are fundamentally malign.

The orthodoxy tells us that marketing executives turn us into anxious yet docile creatures falsely made to believe that the way to find paradise is to buy stuff. A chorus of distinguished commentators, among them Thorstein Veblen, John Kenneth Galbraith, Vance Packard, Ralph Nader, and the philosophers of the Frankfurt School, all condemn the waste, folly, false consciousness and victimhood of consumerist society, which they describe as a conspiracy to force us to labour so that we can purchase the crumbs of pleasure that the system lets fall from the tables of those whose unnecessary products we buy. And in the meantime we are engulfed in waste and pollution as we sit in the blue flicker of television advertisements, eating our unhealthy microwaved TV dinners.

But the evidence in support of this orthodoxy is equivocal. Quite different data suggest that consumers are intelligent in their choices, and that shopping is a profound source of meaning in the modern world. The orthodoxy seems to imply that if only advertisers would leave people alone, they would all begin reading Wittgenstein and listening to Mahler. The fact is, they would not. They want Things; they want Stuff; they want to buy and to own. And as the laws of supply and demand suggest, it is the consumer who leads, while the producers and advertisers scamper after them, supplying the consolations and salvations (religious language springs naturally to mind) that brand names and the joys of ownership provide.

Perhaps therefore consumers' love of consuming is not so contemptible. Defenders of it claim that consuming is the passion and creativity of contemporary life. Through the purchase and possession of Things, they say, we define ourselves, interpret our society, and give our lives coherence. We do not wish to drive a car, but a Ferrari; we do not wish to drink champagne, but Veuve Clicquot; we do not wish to wear a suit, but an Armani suit. Owning them gives us meaning. The language of brands, products and services is the shared language of our community. Logos and advertisements are the cultural emblems of our time, signposts that help us navigate our world and evaluate what we meet in it. Both the language and the images offer what religion once did – a common structure. But as a community bond it is, defenders say, more democratic and equitable. For consumers are not fools, not passive recipients of dogmas taught by a priesthood. They are their own priests; they know what they want, and they are getting it.

Consider the logic of brand names. Why do people buy and wear expensively recognisable brands? Because it gives them a claim to social place, prestige, confidence and purpose. That is the key to consumerism: ownership of precisely these intangibles is what purchase of their tangible vehicles buys.

The argument that consumption is not oppression – that consumers are happy, that consumption is satisfying and gives life meaning – is exhilaratingly robust. But it is hard to resist the thought that, if happiness is what matters, you could achieve the same degree of it more swiftly and economically by putting a suitable drug in the water supply. And it leaves out of account an insight so familiar that it has long been the very cliché of clichés: that of all the things worth having in life, such as kindness, wisdom, and the human affections, none are on offer in the world's shopping-malls.

# PART III
## Amenities and Goods

# Reason

*Reason can wrestle with terrors, and overthrow them.*

EURIPIDES

The conflicts which attract most attention in the news tend either to be political and military in nature, or they involve the struggle between people and the natural environment when, in floods, drought and plague, it turns hostile. But behind these, and detached from them because it is a struggle whose proportions are those of history itself, is another struggle, a profound and consequential one because it shapes long-term human destinies. This is the struggle of ideas, expressing itself in terms of ideologies, politics, and the conceptual frameworks which determine beliefs and moralities. Our understanding of the human situation, and the choices we make in managing the unruly and difficult complexities of social existence, are founded on ideas – usually, ideas systematised into theories. Ultimately it is ideas that drive people to peace or war, which shape the systems under which they live, and which determine how the world's scarce resources are shared among them. Ideas matter; and so therefore does the question of *reason*, by which ideas live or die.

On one view, reason is the armament of ideas, the weapon employed in conflicts between viewpoints. This suggests that in some sense reason is an absolute which, rightly used, can settle disputes and guide us to truth. But reason so understood has always had enemies. One is religion, which claims that revelation from outside the world conveys truths undiscoverable by human enquiry within it. Another is relativism, the view that different truths, different views, different ways of thinking, are all equally valid, and that there is no authoritative standpoint from which they can be adjudicated. The great debates between science and religion are classic expressions of this underlying conflict between competing conceptions of the place and nature of reason.

Most science and philosophy is on the side of the argument which says that reason, despite its imperfections and fallibilities, provides a standard to which competing standpoints must submit themselves. Reason's champions are accordingly hostile to currently fashionable 'postmodernist' views which say that there are authorities more powerful than reason, such as race, tradition, nature, or supernatural entities.

Human traits and values were once thought to be constants, but social and other forms of engineering have turned them into manipulable variables, with the result that we have lost premises from which to reason about aims and means. The power of technology offers us many choices, and thus usurps the fixed starting points of old; so we are afloat, undecided as to values and goals alike. In such circumstances, siren voices grow louder: let us, they say, believe in gods, or potions, or planetary configurations, to find our way. Or, in postmodernist Newspeak, let us recognise that there are only 'discourses', each as valid as any other.

It might be true that human experience is now more fragmented and beset by ironies than it once was, thereby undermining confidence. But still, say the champions of reason, reason remains by far the best guide in the search for knowledge, so despite its failings and limitations we must cling to it.

There are many who reject this view outright. Western civilisation is in crisis, they say, precisely because we believe in reason. We live in thrall to a Utopian ideal of rational society, first mooted by Enlightenment thinkers in the eighteenth century; but the result, contrary to the hopes of such as Voltaire, has not liberated humanity but enslaved it to a bureaucratic corporatism which stumbles, unconstrained by moral purpose, from one disaster to another.

The anti-rationalist argument goes something like this. Enlightenment philosophers sought to rescue people from the arbitrariness of royal or priestly power and to replace it by the rule of reason. But their dream collapsed because of reason's own limitations. All that happened was an increase in the influence of technical elites. The world, in short, became the fiefdom of *managers*. Owners of capital do not control capital; voters do not control politics; everything is run by managers who alone know how to manipulate the structural complexities of society. And the managers' goals – profits, election victories – are not shaped by morality.

This technocratic corporatism applied as much to the now-collapsed Eastern bloc as it does to the West. Indeed the East-West distinction, like that between Left and Right, is not a real distinction at all, such critics argue, but a fiction of the managerial strategy by which the Age of Reason sustains itself.

Simply by listing the problems of contemporary civilisation anyone can make telling points. Reason's critics do so eloquently enough. Politicians, they remind us, get away with speaking literal nonsense because what counts is the manner, not the content, of their utterances. Governments brazenly continue despite their failures because the concept of responsibility no longer applies. Television, advertising, and the worship of artificial heroes such as soap-opera stars blind people to the world's predicament.

These phenomena, and many besides, are symptoms of deep malaise. Worse still are such examples as the arms trade, encouraged by governments who make pious pronouncements about peace and freedom, but who subvert both by their participation in what amounts to legal gun-running. And this is only part of a story in which military establishments flourish, drunk on obsessions with management and technology; and in which many parts of the world are perennially engulfed in war.

Although this compendium of problems contains nothing new, restating them serves to keep us alert. But blame for the world's problems rests not with a concept – still less the Enlightenment's favourite concept of reason – but with people. Reason is merely an instrument which, correctly employed, helps people draw inferences from given premises without inconsistency. Choosing sound premises is what matters, and it is solely a human responsibility. Blaming 'reason' is as meaningful as blaming 'memory' or 'perception'. It was the racism of Nazis, not the logic they applied to put their hatred into effect, which caused the Holocaust.

Do critics mean that the use of reason is bad without qualification? I imagine them at their word-processors, answering the telephone, taking antibiotics for their sore throats, flipping switches to get warmth and light as cold night falls. Are all these products of reason contemptible?

The muddle in the thinking of reason's critics appears when we examine their alternative. They offer us a list of virtues to put in reason's place: one such reads 'spirit, appetite, faith, emotion, intuition, will, experience'. One immediately notes that all but the last, if ungoverned by reason, are exactly the stuff which fuels fanaticism and holy wars. Here lies the poverty of the anti-rationalist's account.

# Education

*Only the educated are free.*

EPICTETUS

Education, and especially 'liberal education', is what makes civil society possible. That means is has an importance even greater than its contribution to economic success, which, alas, is all that politicians seem to think it is for.

To understand the civilising and ethical role of liberal education we need to escape from narrow definitions of 'morality' as conceived in modern times (i.e. since the seventeenth century), and return to a more inclusive classical conception of 'ethics'. As the notion now operates, morality applies just to part of life – to some aspects of human relationships, and to some aspects of character and behaviour. No one thinks that eating bananas is a moral matter, nor whether a person chooses to work in a bank or a building society, or what colour he paints his house. The ancient Greeks thought differently. For them the whole of life is an ethical matter: one lives and does well as a whole person, they said, and both one's flourishing and one's effect on others flow from one's overall character. For this reason life has to be considered – remember Socrates' dictum – and it can only be considered if it is informed. And this is where liberal education comes in.

By 'liberal education' is meant education that includes literature, history and appreciation of the arts, and gives them equal weight with scientific and practical subjects. Education in these pursuits opens the possibility for us to live more reflectively and knowledgeably, especially about the range of human experience and sentiment, as it exists now and here, and in the past and elsewhere. That, in turn, makes us better understand the interests, needs and desires of others, so that we can treat them with respect and sympathy, however different the choices they make or the experiences that have shaped their lives. When respect and sympathy is returned, rendering it mutual, the result is that the gaps which can prompt friction between people, and even war in the end, come to be bridged or at least tolerated. The latter is enough.

The vision is utopian; no doubt there were SS officers who read Goethe and listened to Beethoven, and then went to work in the gas chambers; so liberal education does not automatically produce better people. But it does so far more often than the stupidity and selfishness which arise from lack of knowledge and impoverishment of insight.

Liberal education is a vanishing ideal in the contemporary West, most notably in its Anglophone regions. Education is mainly restricted to the young, and it is no longer liberal education as such but something less ambitious and too exclusively geared to the specific aims – otherwise, of course, very important – of employability. This is a loss; for the aim of liberal education is to produce people who go on learning after their formal education has ceased; who think, and question, and know how to find answers when they need them. This is especially significant in the case of political and moral dilemmas in society, which will always occur and will always have to be negotiated afresh; so members of a community cannot afford to be unreflective and ill-informed if civil society is to be sustainable.

Educating at a high level is expensive, and demands major

investment by a society. But attaining the goal of high-quality education offers glittering prizes. It promises to produce a greater proportion of people who are more than mere foot-soldiers in the economic struggle, by helping them both to get and to give more in their social and cultural experience, and to have lives more fulfilling and participatory both in work and outside it – especially in the amenities of social intercourse, and in the responsibilities of civic and political engagement. People who are better informed and more reflective are more likely to be considerate than those who are – and who are allowed to remain – ignorant, narrow-minded, selfish, and uncivil in the profound sense that characterises so much human experience now.

There is no denying that education is an essential preparation for life and work in an advanced economy. Modern economies require skilled and motivated workers, who can only profit from the opportunities they afford if they are equipped to respond to their demands. So much is now received wisdom.

But a large part of the problem with education is that this connection has become too direct. Aristotle said that we educate ourselves so that we can make noble use of our leisure; this is a view directly opposed to the contemporary belief that we educate ourselves in order to get a job. To that extent the contemporary view distorts the purpose of schooling, by aiming not at the development of individuals as ends in themselves, but as instruments in the economic process.

The key is to distinguish education from training, to recognise that people require both, and to be unabashed about what is involved in the latter. Young children need to be trained in multiplication tables, reading, spelling and writing, exactly as an athlete trains his body: it takes coaching, repetition and practice. When children have acquired skills they can use by reflex, it gives them the confidence and the materials to profit from the next step, which is education proper: the process of learning to think and to know how to find and use information when needed. Above all, education involves refining capacities for judgment and evaluation; Heraclitus remarked that learning is only a means to an end, which is understanding – and understanding is the ultimate value in education.

'Education' etymologically means 'leading out' or 'bringing out', an idea which owes itself to an improbable but long-influential theory put forward by Plato. He believed that we have pre-existing immortal souls which know all things in their disembodied state, but which we forget at birth. On Plato's theory, learning is thus remembering; schooling is the activity of bringing out what is immemorially lodged in our minds. The theory was modified in more sensible directions by later thinkers, who saw education as the evocation of talents and capabilities implicit in the individual, rather than innate knowledge. In one good sense, this is closer to the mark: we still think that human gifts can be helped to flourish if given the right opportunities.

# Excellence

*Uncritical egalitarianism poses a threat to excellence, seen by democratic man as an easily removable cause of envy and exclusion.*

ALEXIS DE TOCQUEVILLE

When Matthew Arnold wrote *Culture and Anarchy* over a hundred years ago, he described the pursuit of excellence in the fostering of culture as 'getting to know, on all the matters that most concern us, the best which has been thought and said in the world, and, through this knowledge, turning a stream of fresh and free thought upon our stock notions and habits.' Arnold was an inspector of schools, and a champion of higher education, and he believed in excellence in education as the way not only to staff the economy but to produce an enculturated society which would live up to the ideal in Aristotle's noble dictum about the educated use of our leisure.

From China to France, every country that is or aspires to be developed has an elite educational stratum, aimed at taking the most gifted students and giving them the best intellectual training possible. In China this is done from an early age, with special schools for the brightest children. In France the system of Hautes Ecoles – superior universities, entry to which is fiercely competitive – creams off the outstanding minds and subjects them to a rigorous discipline. The aim in all cases is to enhance the best in order to gain the highest quality in science, engineering, law, national administration, medicine and the arts.

Few could object to the rationale behind this, save those for whom universal mediocrity is a price worth paying for social equality. But there is a danger to which meritocratic means to the cultivation of excellence – or what should be solely such – fall prey. It is if, after the establishment of the means, merit by itself ceases to be enough, and money and influence become additional criteria. In many, perhaps most, countries in the world, money and influence are the determiners of social advancement, even where meritocratic criteria still apply too: in America money is needed to gain social advantages, in China it helps to be a Party member.

The rich and the well connected are not the kind of elite an education system ought to be fostering. It is easy for popular newspapers and populist politicians to make pejorative use of the term 'elite' to connote these elites of injustice; but they are just as quick to complain if doctors, teachers, or sportsmen playing for national sides fail our highest expectations – if, in short, they are not elite after all, in the proper sense of the term.

Although there are few if any true democracies in the world – most dispensations claiming that name are elective oligarchies – the democratic spirit nevertheless invests Western life, for good and ill both. The good resides in the pressure to treat everyone fairly, the ill resides in the pressure to make everyone alike. This latter is a levelling tendency, a downward thrust, which dislikes excellence because it raises mountains where the nega-tive-democratic spirit wishes to see only plains. But democracy should not aim to reduce people and their achievements to a common denominator; it should aim to raise them, ambitiously and dramatically, as close as possible to an ideal. And that means, among other things, having institutions, especially of learning, which are the best and most demanding of their kind.

# Ambition

*A slave has only one master, an ambitious man as many
masters as there are people he thinks can be useful to him.*

LA BRUYERE

There is understandable pleasure to be taken in the downfall
of the overweening individual who has gambled with truth
and integrity to thrust his way into public notice. A Burmese
proverb says, 'He who takes big paces leaves big spaces', which
readily fill up with trouble. This is a lesson that any number of
collapsed politicians and public figures would do well to learn,
but ambition is a ruthless master, and its votaries easily forget
or ignore the insights that might otherwise save them.

Some might say that it is not desire so much as impatience
which unseats the ambitious person. People in a hurry to be
famous, rich, or both, are apt to cut corners, truth being one of
the easiest to trim. There are certain creatures which run so
fast on the surface of the water that they do not sink, for a time
anyway. But although ambition for worldly success – money,
power, titles – can indeed prompt impatience, and almost always
does, it is only ambition that explains a person's persistence –
even after he has been caught out – in warping facts to conceal
the marches he stole, the parties he gate-crashed, the one-way
streets he drove up the wrong way, and in general the smaller
and greater dishonesties by which he wormed his way, without
a ticket, into life's front row.

It is a risky proceeding; Tacitus put his finger on it when he said, 'Those who aim at empire have no alternative between the highest success and utter downfall.' He was thinking of the bloody history of Rome after Augustus, but the point is general. Ambitious people rely on others to help at crucial moments; but if they leave those others behind in their ascent, they risk turning them into enemies.

But ambition is not a bad thing in itself. Milton called it 'the last infirmity of noble minds', and even those who think it a vice – as is taught in religious moralities of the kind that extol humility and 'knowing one's place' – can agree that though ambition may be a fault in itself, it is often the mother of virtues. Better still is the thought that ambition can be the mother of achievement, leading to scientific discovery, works of art, enhancement of the public good. A desire to be ranked with the great figures of the past can be a good emulation, if it recognises what it takes. Worthy ambition, in short, is responsible ambition, because it is prepared to pay the costs of attainment. Mere ambition wants to leap high without effort, and looks for easy ladders.

The difference is well illustrated by the contrast – to employ a familiar example – between the person who says he 'wishes to be a writer' and the person who says he 'wishes to write'. The former desires to be pointed out at cocktail parties, the latter is prepared for the long, solitary hours at a desk; the former desires a status, the latter a process; the former desires to be, the latter to do.

It remains true that most ambition is not noble aspiration but mere 'wild ambition' which, says Dryden, 'loves to slide, not stand,/ And Fortune's ice prefers to Virtue's land.' It is the ambition which consumes other people, and veracity, and trust, and eventually itself. But only, of course, if it is found out; which some seem to think is the only sin it is really possible to commit.

# Acting

*Good actors are good because of the things they can tell us without talking.*

CEDRIC HARDWICKE

It seems to be a human need, because it is a human universal, to tell – or more tellingly, to enact – stories about human experience. There are many reasons for this, apart from the entertainment value. We watch or read tales about lives like our own, and lives unlike our own, to understand ourselves better, to understand other possibilities better, and sometimes to escape both. A potent way of doing so is through performance, especially in film and theatre, which reprise one of the most ancient of the arts, namely, storytelling as a live performance. One easily imagines humanity's remote ancestors gathered round the fire at night to retell legends about gods, heroes and the hunt, either dancing and singing them, or watching poets recount them in the footlight of the flames under a proscenium of stars, gesticulating and changing voices to suit the story, encouraged by a firelit ring of intent spectators. The first poets and historians were actors by necessity.

Professional actors are not merely playwrights' mouthpieces. They have the same relation to the text of a play as a musician does to a composer's score. They must grasp its possibilities of meaning, and they must know what an audience understands by another's ways of saying and seeming, moving and doing.

The least of their craft thus demands skills of interpretation and representation. By connecting them an actor mirrors the world, and makes audiences believe they see truth in the reflection.

Shakespeare was fond of the convertible insights that the stage is a microcosm of the world, and the world a macrocosm of the stage. When the world's a stage, he famously said, all its inhabitants are players, their lives a series of parts from the infant 'mewling and puking in its nurse's arms' to the super-annuate entering 'second childishness and mere oblivion'. But people are actors in more ways than this. We talk of the different roles we play, many of them simultaneously, as children and parents, colleagues and friends, customers and consumers, spectators and participants. We adjust our behaviour according to the company or the circumstances we find ourselves in. As a result we may play a variety of parts in a single day, some very different from others – and yet all of them are ourselves, all of them express facets of our identities, which are therefore more multiple, protean and evolving than we realise, even if the sum of their interactions yields a personality that is, within a range of variability, stable in its appearance to the outside world – like the sound of a chord made up of many notes.

The acting of roles comes naturally in ordinary life, because ordinary life demands it; but it helps to know this latter fact, so that one can be prepared not just to play one's part when required, but to act a part if required. The words 'acting' and 'action' have the same root in the Latin verb *ago, agere, egi, actum*, 'to do, to drive, to lead'. To play one's part, to have a role, is therefore to be active rather than passive; it is to take charge of oneself, and to make a difference of one's own choosing.

Thinking of a person as a troupe of actors explains much. It explains the difficulty each individual has in defining a sense of self, at least until the members of the troupe have each had their turn on life's stage. It explains the mistake in thinking that there is a royal route – for example, psychotherapy – which could help one to find the truth about oneself, for its shows that there are many routes to many truths about oneself, and at least several of them have to be travelled before the relation between those truths can be understood. And it explains why, when instructed to 'be yourself', it is so hard to comply; unless what comes closest to a central self is the one you are when you are unaware of yourself, and when you are happy without knowing it.

# Art

*You use a glass mirror to see your face; you use works of art to see your soul.*

GEORGE BERNARD SHAW

A survey was once conducted to find out what teenagers think of museums, art galleries and the theatre. Unsurprisingly, it discovered that most of them dislike such places. It seems they think them boring, and associate them with 'rich old people'. The survey concluded that if homes of the arts offered more cafés and leisure activities, and if performances were shorter, teenagers might be more inclined to go.

With luck, no one will ever take any notice of this survey. It says nothing new, for things have always been thus. If galleries and theatres started trying to attract teenagers they would fail, while at the same time alienating their natural constituencies. The arts have always been, and always will be, avocations for minorities. 'Art teaches nothing, except the significance of life', said Henry Miller; and most people never get to the second half of the sentence.

The good news is that as populations increase, so do the numbers in minorities. As a result, more people than ever before in history now enjoy the arts. Exhibitions are crowded, concerts fully booked. And therefore more people discover the richness of pleasure and insight that the arts give. 'Thanks to art,' said Proust, 'instead of seeing one world, our own, we see it multiplied, and as many original artists as there are, so many worlds are at our disposal.'

Philistinism is not universal among teenagers, but it is a professional phase with many. Their supposed contempt for the arts is not really about the arts, but about themselves: they are not always ready for what the arts offer. Some of them come to feel the need for more content, more juice in things, and that is when the arts invite them. 'Art comes to you proposing frankly to give nothing but the highest quality to your moments as they pass,' said Pater. Once accepted, that invitation can never thereafter be refused.

Pieties, unlike clichés, carry no guarantee of truth: but there is a familiar one about the arts which does. It is that when a thoughtful and receptive sensibility engages with the arts, it is nourished by them, and learns from them, not least how to be discerning: 'It is only the dullness of the eye that makes any two things seem alike,' Pater also said, and the idea of the uniqueness and particularity of things carries over from a painting or a moment of dance to a moral circumstance or an individual's suffering. In that way art civilises too, because it is, as Shaw says, a mirror for souls.

Perhaps the young find it hard to appreciate the arts because the arts are themselves always youthful. 'Art is never didactic, does not take kindly to facts, is helpless to grapple with theories, and is killed outright by a sermon,' said Agnes Repplier, and she could have put 'youth' for 'art' at the sentence's head. Many mistakenly think that art must be approached in one's mental Sunday best; that it lacks laughs; that it changes nothing. The opposite is true, and those who discover this fact are infinitely the richer for it.

# Health

*When we are well, we all have good advice for those who are ill.*

TERENCE

Two thousand years ago Plutarch counselled a moderate diet, exercise and restful sleep as the basis of good health. Nothing has since happened to humankind to render his advice obsolete. But plenty has happened to make all three harder to get. People dig their graves with their teeth, as the saying has it; their muscles and organs grow soft and fatty from physical idleness, and stress destroys their rest, so that they toss and groan in their beds unless a drug blunts their disquiet – sleeping pills or alcohol. For this disease ('dis-ease') there is a simple but powerful prescription, offered by Bertrand Russell; the key to happiness, he said, is to worry about things only when relevant. If you cannot do anything about your overdraft at three in the morning, stop thinking about it until you can.

There are, as usual, contrasting opinions about the kind of advice offered by Plutarch. A Spanish proverb says, 'If you would live in health, be old early.' That is contradicted by G. B. Shaw's cheerful urging to use your health 'even to the point of wearing it out. That is what it is for. Spend all you have before you die; and do not outlive yourself.' Shaw was a teetotal vegetarian who lived to be bright as a button in his nineties, which hardly qualifies him to prompt others along Dorian Gray's route.

More people go to doctors now, proportionally, than ever before; and we are healthier and longer-lived than previous generations. Which way round does the connection go? Are people better for seeing doctors more often, or are we better because of diet and hygiene, but less tolerant of minor ailments? Some suggest that doctors have taken over from priests as comforters and confessors; the Prozac tablet is the wafer of salvation. It seems that about a third of surgery visits are related to psychological difficulties.

The words 'health' and 'wholeness' come from the same root – old Saxon and Early English words like *hool*, *heil* and *hail* (as in 'hale and hearty') meaning 'unwounded, entire, sound'. These concepts in turn echo the ancient idea that health is a form of bodily and mental integrity, in which nothing is missing or amiss: a balance, as the ancients had it, between the wet, cold, hot and dry 'humours'. They constructed a system of medicine on this idea, based on prevention first and cure by diet second. Most famous among them was Galen, physician to Marcus Aurelius, who began life as a *therapeutes* (an attendant) on the god of healing, Asclepius, and travelled the Roman world gathering medical lore. After serving as surgeon to the gladiators, he taught anatomy and physiology, and practised animal vivisection for research. He taught that the fundamental principle of life is air, and said that venous and arterial blood constitute two different circulatory systems.

There is no entirely satisfactory definition of health, because of its subjective character, but one good suggestion is that it is what you have when you do not notice that you have it. To say this is not, despite appearances, to agree with Oliver Wendell Holmes's claim, 'If you mean to keep as well as possible, the less you think about your health the better,' which is bad advice; health deserves thought, and a modicum of care: for prevention is best, early cure is second best, and both require a sensible watchfulness. Health is not an end in itself, it is the principal instrument for the enjoyment of life: 'Health exists for life, and life exists for the love of music and beautiful things,' said Chesterton; and he is right on both counts.

# Leisure

*The highest pleasure to be got out of freedom, and having nothing to do, is labour.*

MARK TWAIN

Many people plan their holidays by leafing through magazines to ponder advertisements offering everything from Andes pony trekking to Zimbabwean big-game viewing. The majority end by choosing beaches in the middle of the alphabet – Majorca, Malaga, Morocco. Most of these, in turn, think of holidays as paradigmatic times of leisure, by which they mean opportunity for relaxation not just of body and mind but – even if only in the form of a little self-indulgence – of morals too: for holidays and moral holidays go together like cakes and ale.

And in one good sense of the word 'leisure', they are right; for it derives from the Middle French *leisir* meaning 'to be permitted', which in turn stems from the Latin *licere*, from which comes 'licence'. So leisure is licence, freedom – specifically, freedom from work and duties, allowing one to be at ease, to turn to pleasure, to lay aside obligations and rules. A good example of the licence afforded by leisure is holiday romance, apt to flare and die with equal suddenness. There is a pleasing irony in the fact that holidays are in this respect an opportunity for sin, for 'holiday' once meant 'holy day'.

This conception of leisure is now the dominant one. It is made to contrast straightforwardly with work; and the reflex view is that it is far more desirable than work. In his famous 'theory of the leisure class' Thorstein Veblen claimed that a life of leisure is the highest and most beautiful kind. Most who dream about winning the lottery envisage joining that class by quitting work and taking it easy thereafter – beachcombing, playing golf, travelling, 'listening to the tap leak and the crabgrass grow – and leaving them so', to paraphrase Marya Mannes.

And yet leisure could only be better than work (apart from especially grinding or drudging work) if it were also a life of activity, because mere idleness, after a time, is burdensome. 'Absence of occupation is not rest; a mind quite vacant is a mind distressed', wrote William Cowper, wagging his finger but speaking truth. Aristotle's fine sentiment about well-used leisure construes it as an opportunity to enjoy what makes us flourish: to pursue the arts, to reflect, to deepen understanding, to further friendships, and to pursue excellence. If work is concerned with securing life's necessities, leisure is concerned with cultivating its amenities. It is a commonplace that high civilisation requires leisure, because both the production and the enjoyment of art need time and psychological space, which the harshness of subsistence labour practically excludes.

These lofty remarks invite a reminder: that leisure has typically been the privilege of a few carried on the sweated backs of many. Some aesthetes repine – but only for a moment – at the melancholy reflection that beauty is rooted in suffering. But the happy fact is that civilisation-producing leisure has not always been an aristocratic monopoly. It was once an organic part of work. In the season of plenty – which, paradoxically, was winter, when the grain and the salted pork were safely stored – darkness and hard frosts kept people indoors, making things; including songs, stories, carvings and textiles. From this change of occupation which the flux of seasons enforced was born painting, poetry, theatre and music. From it also came science, in reflection on experience gathered during the working parts of the year.

The kind of holidays people usually take are not really – so these thoughts suggest – exercises in leisure, but in rest. If they were longer than two or three weeks they would get boring, and would make us hungry for mental stimulus. So viewed, leisure is not the opposite of work, it is – as Mark Twain and Aristotle both suggest – something better: the opportunity to work for higher ends.

# Peace

*Peace is better and safer than hopes of victory.*

LIVY

Like most commonplaces, those about peace are usually forgotten in times of peace. And like most commonplaces, they are profoundly true. Peace is the condition required for education, and the arts, and the formation of human relationships. It is when music can be made, crops sown and gathered, houses and monuments built. Peace gives a society time for reflection; which is where most good things have their start. 'Fair peace is becoming to man,' says Ovid, 'fierce anger belongs to the beasts.'

Perhaps unsurprisingly, not everyone agrees. The usually mild-mannered A. N. Whitehead, who wrote *Principia Mathematica* with Bertrand Russell, said, 'The deliberate aim of Peace easily passes into its bastard substitute, Anaesthesia.' He echoes a view long held among extollers of the warrior virtues that war is better for the human spirit. Bewailing what he saw as Rome's effeteness, Juvenal wrote, 'Now we suffer the woes of long peace; luxury, more savage than war, has smothered us.' Even pacifists acknowledge that war and the threat of war drive technological and scientific change faster; at the beginning of the Second World War some air forces still had biplanes in active service (in the RAF, the sturdy Gloucester Gladiator), replaced at its end by long-range missiles, jet fighters and atomic bombs. This seems to prove Adorno's dispiriting conclusion that all human progress can be summed up as the advance from the spear to the guided missile, showing that though we have grown cleverer through time, we have certainly not grown wiser.

But when we see just who these martial sentiments most persuade – 'Mankind has grown strong in eternal struggles and it will only perish through eternal peace,' said Adolf Hitler – we might be inclined to think that a lean peace is, after all, better than a fat war. And it prompts a distinction: between peace understood as the condition of a state or, more generally, a society, in which it is neither internally nor externally engaged in armed conflict; and personal peace, in which an individual is on good terms with those around him, and free from anxieties within.

Personal peace thus mirrors social peace in having both external and internal aspects. External peace is always desirable. Because of the opportunities it gives and its restorative powers, internal peace is more than desirable, it is necessary: but only at times. As millstones require grit, so the mind requires problems to solve, difficulties to overcome, challenges to face. 'The only condition of peace in this world,' said Oliver Wendell Holmes, meaning inner personal peace, 'is to have no ideas, or at least' – now meaning external personal peace – 'not to express them.' In certain traditions, internal peace is the highest goal of man: 'He knows peace who has given up desire,' says the Bhagavadgita. But why give up desire?

# Reading

*How many a man has dated a new era in his life from the reading of a book!*

THOREAU

It seems that some doctors prescribe books instead of medications to patients suffering from depression, stress and anxiety. The patients are referred to a bibliotherapist – yes: bibliotherapist – who give patients reading lists suited to their conditions. The treatment's inspiration was the observation by librarians that borrowers are apt to say, on returning a book, that it did them good by making them laugh or by distracting them from their troubles.

There are almost too many things to say about this amazing fact. Cynics will ask, What sort of pass are we in that people need a doctor's prescription to prompt them to read? When did we forget that reading is, for a thousand reasons, one of the chief resources of life? Will doctors turn to prescribing dinner for the hungry and sleep for the tired as the next step in the medicalisation of human existence, or as a response to the supine inability of people to think and act for themselves?

There is a tincture of justice in these exclamations, but it is not appropriately directed at doctors. It should rather be directed at the failure of our culture to show people what rich deposits of pleasure and usefulness, and what expansion of horizons, are to be found in reading. An education in reading includes guidance – very easy to give; it takes five minutes (much less if you say, 'Ask a librarian,' which is excellent advice) – on how to find any required book or kind of book. And just a little experience as a reader grants access to the great country where one flies as an eagle over the history, comedy, tragedy and variety of human experience, at every point garnering much, if the reading is attentive, from the abundance on offer.

The key is 'attentive'. The best thing any education can bequeath is habits of reflection and questioning. Reading can be a passive affair, an entertainment leaving no impression on the mind beyond a pleasant present distraction. Many books are skilfully written to demand no more, and there is nothing wrong with that. But for anything more, reading has to be an activity, not a passivity. It is hard to define what makes good books good, because good books come in so many different kinds, but one thing common to most of them is that they make readers think and feel, elevating or disturbing them, and making them see the world a little differently as a result. In short, they elicit the activity in active reading. 'We find little in a book but what we put there,' Joseph Joubert said. 'But in great books, the mind finds room to put many things.'

Reading does not automatically make people wiser or better. When it has that effect it is because readers have done the work themselves, quarrying the materials from their response to the printed page. But apart from practical experience of life, which is everyone's chief tutor, scarcely anything compares with books as the mine where that quarrying can begin. To read is to enter other points of view; it is to be an invisible observer of circumstances which might never be realised in one's own life; it is to meet people and situations exceeding in kind and number the possibilities open to individual experience. As a result, reading not only promotes self-understanding, it equips one with insights into needs, interests and desires that one might never share but which motivate others, in this way enabling one to understand, and tolerate, and even to sympathise with, other people's concerns. As an extension of how this informs one's behaviour towards others, it is also the basis for civil community and the brotherhood of man.

I keep a photograph on my desk of the Philosophical Library in the Strahof Monastery in Prague. Taken from the upper gallery, it captures the tranquil beauty of that deep room, filled with light from the clerestory windows in the right-hand wall. The photograph shows one long bar of sunshine lying across a tier of book-shelves, illuminating the richness of the leather bindings ranked there. Below, on the ground floor, three desks are disposed at comfortable intervals, among them an ingenious reading wheel any scholar would envy.

The scene is wonderfully expressive of everything to do with books, and the reading of books; with study and thought, with books as the distillations of time and man's endeavours – even of the world itself, brought into reflective equilibrium and clothed in quietness and retreat. If, off to one side, there were a closet with a bed in it and wherewithal to make tea, one would not mind being locked in there, and the key thrown away.

A cynic might proclaim this beautiful and evocative library a mere dead mortuary of books, a past curiosity for dull-eyed tourists to glance at, a selling-point for the postcards that now represent its only product. But I think it is a work of art, and represents something opposed to the uneasy, fickle, failing norm of most human life and its compromises.

A library is like a hive storing honey, part of the best, sweetest and most nourishing exudate of human experience. A commentator on Vergil's *Georgics* Book IV, which tells of honey-bees and lost love, remarked that only four things withstand time – gold, sunlight, amber and honey. Some archaeologists digging in Greece once came across an ancient amphora filled to the brim with honey over 2000 years old. They took a little each day to spread on their bread at breakfast. After a time they noticed that there was something at the bottom of the amphora. When they looked, they found that it was the body of an infant.

It is an extraordinarily touching thought that the mourning parents of this child, so long ago, buried it in honey to preserve it forever. The action speaks of great wealth, and great love.

# Memory

*Memory tells us not what we choose, but what it pleases.*

Forgetfulness, as Plutarch says, 'transforms every occurrence into a non-occurrence'. His view rests on the standard assumption that memory is an organ of perception into the past, much as the eyes and other senses are organs of perception into the present. As such, it counts as a source of knowledge, connecting us with previous events by the traces they have left in our minds. For proponents of this view, the causal links between originating experiences and present memories form a bridge to past time. The promise of this view seems great, because there are no other comparable roads into the past; all the documents and remains used as evidence by historians are things that exist in the present, and their testimony is often ambiguous.

Unfortunately, to regard memory as a source of knowledge is a risky commitment. Memories occur in the present, just like the historians' documents, and genuine memories are often indistinguishable from mistaken ones or from mere imaginings. There is no contradiction in regarding a given mental experience as a memory, with there yet being no reliable connection between it and a past event. In the nature of the case it is impossible to verify a memory fully, because it is impossible to set the memory side by side with the event that putatively caused it, thus testing its accuracy.

Even genuine memories can be notoriously unreliable; no good court of law accepts the uncorroborated recollections of a witness as conclusive. Support from the memory of someone else might help, but only to a limited degree; for memory is subjective, and as the police know to their frustration, two witnesses to the same event can give very different accounts of it. Memories can change, adding and losing details, distorting out of shape under the pressure of time.

Although memory is an unreliable source of knowledge about the past, its role both in intelligence and self-identity is unquestionable. Intelligence crucially involves memory; inability to make use of acquired information and past experience is a severe limitation on performance of mental and practical tasks alike. Similarly, memory is crucial to self-identity; when a person suffers memory loss, one of the most distressing concomitants is loss of the sense of self. On some views, what makes a person the same person through life is the accumulating set of memories he carries with him. When these are lost, he ceases to be that person and becomes someone else, new and as yet unformed.

And yet it seems that too much memory is equally bad. In his story 'Funes the Memorious' Jorge Luis Borges describes the agony of an individual who can forget nothing, and who is tortured by the burden of complete recall. In a prescient remark made just before the Holocaust, Sholem Asch wrote, 'Not the power to remember, but its very opposite, the power to forget, is necessary to our existence,' a truth later acknowledged by many survivors as an important part of the healing required before the proper work of remembering could begin.

Aeschylus called memory 'the mother of the Muses', according it thereby the role of foundation of all the arts. The Greeks sometimes called the Muses 'Mneiai', which means 'the

Remembrances'. In this sense memory is not individual rec-
ollection but collective tradition, and Aeschylus's point is that
without tradition in this sense there would be no literature or
music, no history or science, for all these pursuits are cumu-
lative, depending for their progress on lessons learned and mistakes rectified beforehand. That is one reason why history, as the
attempt to achieve an agreed collective memory – a tradition – is
so important; without an understanding of antecedents, we are
always in danger of reinventing the wheel, sometimes in any
shape but round.

Tradition differs from individual memory in one very important respect: the latter can be true or false, but the former is
neither – it just is what it is.

It is always a mistake to underestimate how long it takes for
mankind to understand the traumas it has suffered, especially
the self-inflicted ones. In the half-century since the end of the
Second World War the facts of the Nazi attempt to exterminate
Europe's Jews have become a matter of detailed knowledge, and
the massive body of historical data relating to it has received
meticulous analysis by scholars. So vast an event as the organised murder of millions, carried out on an industrial scale, is
impossible to hide from history's prying eyes. The perpetrators'
perverse sense of order, and the many witnesses and survivors
inevitably left by a project of such terrible ambition, have
together worked to keep the evidence in existence. That is
one reason why revisionist attempts to persuade us that the
Holocaust did not happen, or was 'not as bad as is claimed', are
futile: the mountain of facts is as huge as the horror it records.

Yet the psychological task of grasping the Holocaust is made
not easier but harder by the systematic analysis of the facts.
The more we know, down to details of individual men on
specifiable dates in precise locations shooting or gassing to death
other human beings – men and women, the elderly, children,

babies too small to walk – in dozens, or hundreds, or thousands – the more our sense of moral perplexity and disorientation grows, and our revulsion and pity interfere with the task of comprehension. One thing we know is that we have to keep working hard at severing the Hydra's heads of racism, nationalism, and cultural and religious bitterness which everywhere relentlessly threaten – for as recent history has shown in the Balkans, Ulster and Kashmir, East Timor, Tibet and Rwanda, the same dangers always lurk.

This is why many Europeans dream of uniting their continent, to reduce the conditions for war and what can happen under its cover. It is why the human rights movement exists, with its slow progress towards international agencies capable of enforcing the conventions agreed by the party states of the United Nations. These historic movements are responses to the Holocaust, and the fact that their progress stutters and stumbles is a worrying sign of mankind's short memory and blind self-interest, faults which even so gross an insult to humanity as the Holocaust seems unable to overcome. Humanity does well therefore to keep memory of the Holocaust vivid, until its recurrence has become an impossibility.

# History

*To remain ignorant of what happened before you were born is to remain always a child.*

CICERO

What is history? There is ambiguity in the very name. 'History' can either mean past events, or writings about past events. But what if the former is a creation of the latter? The past, after all, has ceased to exist. Here in the present we find documents and other objects which, we suppose, survive from the past, and we weave interpretations round them. These objects, and our interpretations, belong to the present. If history is different narratives constructed in the present, is it any wonder that historians disagree among themselves?

The idea that the past is another country, spread out 'behind' us, which we could visit if we had a time-machine, is naive. Yet our realism is offended by the claim that the past is created in the present, and we oppose the latitude thus accorded those who, for example, deny that the Holocaust happened.

What, then, is history? Is it an art that creates, or a science that discovers? Either way, is there – can there be – such a thing as historical truth? And if so, to what extent can it be known?

'History' derives from the ancient Greek word *historia*, meaning 'enquiry'. But even in antiquity the fatal ambiguity arose; by the fourth century BC the *historikos* – the reciter of stories – had supplanted the *historeon* – the enquirer. Into which category should we place the great early historians – Herodotus, Thucydides, Polybius, Livy, Sallust, Tacitus?

They too understood the problem. Thucydides attacked Herodotus for his expansive and anecdotal history – made up of an artfully arranged collection of stories, facts, legends and speculations – of the great East-West struggle between Persia and Greece. Thucydides began his history of the Peloponnesian War with the claim that history should be 'contemporary history', restricting itself to what can be verified by personal observation. He served in the Athenian army, and wrote as he fought.

Art outweighed science in most historical writing as far as the Renaissance. But from the seventeenth century the possibility of scientific history emerged from work on sources. Benedictine monks established principles for authenticating medieval manuscripts, thus inaugurating the systematic treatment of materials. By the time Leopold von Ranke (1795–1886) summoned historians to record the past 'as it actually happened', the project seemed possible.

Other 'Positivists' claimed that there are inductively discoverable historical laws. The great Victorian, John Stuart Mill, agreed, adding that psychological laws count among them. On this view history is truly a science: good data and general laws pave the way to objective truth.

But the Positivists were opposed by the Idealists, such as Wilhelm Dilthey (1833–1911). Under the influence of Kant and Hegel, they argued that whereas natural science studies phenomena from the outside, social science does so from the inner perspective of human experience. History accordingly is a reconstruction of the past by 'intellectual empathy' with our forebears.

Dilthey said that history is nevertheless objective, because the products of human experience – books and art – belong to the public domain. But his fellow Idealists disagreed; Benedetto Croce (1866–1952) wrote that history is subjective because the historian himself is always present in its construction. As James Baldwin put it, 'People are trapped in history, and history is trapped in them.' These ideas constitute the philosophy of history. They are not works of history, nor of historiography (discussion of historical techniques). But nor are they works of philosophical history, exemplified by those grand theories of history's metaphysical significance offered by Hegel, Marx, Spengler and Toynbee. These latter claim that history manifests patterns, and moves towards an ultimate goal. Positivist history is an attempt to escape the seductions of such a view, by seeking for facts. Idealist arguments show that this aim is easier to state than achieve.

Such cases as the attempt by 'Holocaust deniers' to minimise the Nazi assault on European Jewry, in turn, show that the argument matters.

At the same time it is true that, in general, people are only too pleased to be led. Because of weakness, ignorance and laziness – laziness above all – most would rather leave it to others to take decisions. Seneca observed that what makes people unhappy is not being given orders, but being made to do things against their will. Because few relish resolving complicated questions or making important choices, it is not duty or obedience they dislike, but being obliged to take responsibility.

Some say that a leader who is kind, considerate and prepared to lead by example, will be most cheerfully and loyally followed. But it is equally true, as Homer says in Alexander Pope's translation, that 'the leader mixing with the vulgar host / Is in the common mass of matter lost'. This suggests that a fine balance is needed between the degree of distance and condescension (in the literal sense of that term) a leader should observe. But equally wise heads point out that when leadership involves – as it often does – unpopular decisions and hard actions, what used to be a cheerfully loyal following becomes more disaffected than one with which the leader had a merely pragmatic relationship.

According to some views, the chief reason why history is littered with demagogues is the laziness and weakness of the mass already alluded to. People in the mass appear to relish a firm leader, a guide, a Führer. They think that his iron resolve will protect them from the further collapse – one that every generation believes imminent – of their social, moral and economic order, whose golden period existed in the past (or perhaps coincided with their own early childhood). The roots of this impulse lie deep in mankind's evolutionary history. Ethologists distinguish two kinds of social structure among monkeys and primates: the 'agonic' in which order is kept in the troop by violence, and the 'hedonic' in which social ranking is determined by which animal shows off best. When an alpha male baboon goes into a dominance display, other baboons flee. When an alpha male chimpanzee does so, the others settle down to watch. Human society mixes the two; policemen and pop-stars illustrate the baboon and chimpanzee parts respectively. A leader of the demagogic variety combines both menace and theatre, as witness the Nuremberg rallies, and in that sense he is a paradigm for all aspiring leaders; which prompts the question: who, therefore, needs them – or at least, the baboon part of them?

# Travel

*Many shall run to and fro, and knowledge shall be increased.*

DANIEL 12:4

Sir Richard Burton, a great traveller and adventurer, remarked that 'travellers, like poets, are an angry race.' That might be true, but it does not alter the fact that travel is a source of many benefits. Chiefly, there is the fact that people know too little about their own country if they know no other. Travel is a rich source of information and altered perspectives, as everyone understands; both, apart from being intrinsically valuable, have the practical merit of placing one's own locale, and its inhabitants, in an informatively fresh light. They suggest possibilities yet undreamed of, improvements previously unimagined, and reasons for satisfaction with home: all worth having. In the past travellers spread news and knowledge by bringing home observations from abroad. They told tall tales sometimes, and sometimes brought the plague; but most of mankind's technological and agricultural improvements resulted from the travels of individuals. Until recent times such travels were most often an intrepid because dangerous adventure.

The benefit of knowledge accrues only to the true traveller, not the tourist – a vital distinction. The traveller is an active being. He has understood Dr Johnson's remark that 'in travelling a man must carry knowledge with him, if he would bring knowledge home.' He goes to look and see, to be taught, to sympathise and understand. The tourist is not an active being, he is passive; he expects to be carried abroad, conveyed from the airport to his hotel, provided with entertainments and refreshments, and protected from foreign annoyances. He does not learn the rudiments of the local language before going, relying instead on his package-tour guide or on speaking English loudly. The traveller seeks adventure, not least of the mind; the tourist expects nice things to happen to him. To give him his due, the tourist has gone abroad expecting differences; but as a spectator, not a student, of them; and for that one might as well watch television. 'As a member of an escorted tour,' Temple Fielding remarked, 'you don't even have to know that the Matterhorn isn't a tuba.'

Sceptics about travel have probably been tourists at heart. Horace, usually so astute ('the young love Ovid, the mature love Horace'), grumbled that 'they change their climate, not their souls, who rush across the sea,' a dictum which is false as applied to travellers, although it could be adapted to define tourism. Emerson was of Horace's mind: 'travelling is a fool's paradise,' he wrote; 'we owe to our first journey the discovery that place is nothing.' His remark is astonishing given what he learned from his own travels. For example, in Italy he met Walter Savage Landor, who memorably said to him, 'A man must slaughter his hundred oxen, despite not knowing whether they will be eaten by gods or flies.' To hear such a tremendous remark from the poet's own lips would repay crossing any number of oceans.

When Thomas Jefferson, third President of the United States, was travelling in Europe during the 1780s, he came to two conclusions: that travel is best done alone, because one reflects more on what one sees; and that travel makes men wiser but less happy. His great contemporary Goethe took the opposite view. The right travelling companion is another pair of eyes,

# Privacy

*Among crowds, on our travels, even at banquets, our inner thoughts give us a place of privacy.*

QUINTILIAN

It is a feature of contemporary life that people in public positions have become victims of an insatiable mass desire to turn everything into soap opera. By definition, celebrities are people famous for being famous, and the price of being famous is having *paparazzi* crowding your doorstep and rummaging in your rubbish bins. In fact it has long been thus; a century ago Samuel Butler wrote, 'There is a photographer in every bush, going about like a roaring lion seeking whom he may devour.'

That is what Charles Parnell must have felt when in 1886 the *Pall Mall Gazette* revealed his adulterous visits to Mrs Kitty O'Shea in Eltham, precipitating a huge scandal. The *News of the World* had been entertaining its Sunday readership with details of murders and divorces since 1843. In this they follow ancient tradition; Socrates' private life – especially his sexual interests – was made the subject of public speculation by Aristoxenus, and it had long before been revealed that his wife Xantippe nagged him.

When Oscar Wilde left Reading Gaol in May 1897 he had to be smuggled to the railway station to avoid waiting reporters; on seeing a flowering bush for the first time in two years he threw open his arms and exclaimed, 'Oh beautiful world!' –

whereupon a warder whispered, 'Now, Mr Wilde! You mustn't give yourself away like that. You're the only man in England who would talk like that in a railway station.'

Privacy matters to the famous because they have lost it. We usually only place the right value on things when we have lost them. People in the unremitting glare of the public gaze – even those, like Princess Diana, who hungrily court that gaze, and manipulate it and define themselves by it – quickly find themselves desperate for privacy. They just as quickly feel the need for something often confused with privacy but quite different from it, namely, solitude. Solitude is the welcome physical absence of others (loneliness – different yet again – is the unwelcome psychological absence of others). Privacy has nothing to do with the absence or presence of others; it is having aspects of one's life, feelings and activities known and reserved only to oneself or the few to whom one chooses to reveal them.

Privacy is a necessity, no less than food and drink. Part of its importance is that it helps us keep at least some control over how we appear to the world. Most people need to be liked and accepted, for the usual psychological and practical reasons. It could be awkward or even disabling to have all one's sentiments and personal habits publicly known, especially the embarrassing or conventionally unacceptable ones. Again, at their first outset one's endeavours are generally too immature to bear the scrutiny of others; they need to be nourished in privacy before they are ready for exposure.

Few people can function without a private life. In the circle of family or chosen friends people can relax their guards, be themselves, express themselves naturally. A hidden microphone, or a telephoto lens that captures their intimate contacts with others, is a violent theft of what is central to their wellbeing. Even lovers need to retain a certain privacy from each other; to be unable to have secrets is to be bereft of a self. To Proust, as to others, the private, innermost self – the *moi profond* – is and should be as much a secret to oneself as to others.

In the wake of tabloid mania for intruding on celebrities' lives has come discussion of Rights to Privacy. The dilemma is that pieties about privacy can sometimes be a mask for abuse, and in a free society the right of the press to expose hidden abuses is as important as the individual's right to be left alone. The question is: where is the line between legitimate exposure and psychological rape? Unsatisfactory as it seems, it is better to draw it after the event, and for individual cases, rather than to have a blanket law. So invasion of privacy is the price of accountability. But the tabloid newspapers usually go too far, and they know it; and destroy good things in the process.

# Family

'Family values' is a mantric phrase in political debate which represents a victory of sorts for the religious Right on both sides of the Atlantic. But the more one examines the ideas behind talk of the 'traditional family' and 'family values', the more muddled and tendentious they appear.

For one thing, there is nothing traditional about the 'traditional family'. The paradigm is a legally married adult male-female couple with two children in a three-bedroomed semi. This 'nuclear family' is a product of the industrial age, and no older than the nineteenth century. In all societies beforehand, and in most non-Western societies now, families are larger and more diffuse groups, typically embracing more than two generations, in which child-care is as often carried out by relatives as parents who, because they are of economically active age, tend to be out at work all day.

In these larger groups the dynamics of personal relationships work very differently from those in the claustrophobic and introverted modern nuclear family, the pressures within which and on which explain its dramatic unsuccess as a social unit. The majority of nuclear families fail: forty per cent end in divorce, and one can only guess at the soul-stunting compromises and struggles on the basis of which many of the rest survive.

One of the most striking comments on the 'traditional family' is that as soon as its economically active members can afford it, they purchase its extension into a genuinely traditional family – with a cleaner, a mother's help, an au pair, or a nanny; in short, additional members to share and diffuse the burdens and to change the nature of the relationships within the group. Until Victorian times the word 'family' included the servants too, and it is a confident prediction that there is no family anywhere today which, if it can afford it, does not have 'help' of some kind, replacing the lost larger structure more natural to the basis of human domestic community.

The associated phrase 'family values' is shorthand for a pre-packaged moral outlook which is hostile to sex, drugs, abortion and homosexuality, and anxious to keep 'young people' sexually ignorant and inactive until marriage, which must be monogamous and lifelong, and which must obtain only between a man and a woman. The relation between 'traditional family' and 'family values' lies in the sentimentalised conception of social control that extollers of the latter hope will be exercised by the former.

Some nuclear families are of course blissfully happy, but it would be a mistake to ignore the opposite truth in Strindberg's attack on the family as 'home of all social evils' and Butler's pessimistic belief that 'more unhappiness comes from this source than any other'. In denying that families work best when their nature and structure is freely chosen by their participants and respected by the outside world, no matter what form they take, upholders of 'traditional values' militate against happiness. People need company to share burdens and pleasures, to give solace and enjoy intimacy, to receive and express love, and to nurture the next generation. The nuclear family is far from being the only or best way such relationships can flourish; and

in the variety of alternative arrangements – gay couples, single-
or multiple-parent families, extended households – 'family
values' are not always or even often to the point.

For any family, though, the quoted proverb applies; you do
best to run it as you would cook a small fish – which is, the
Chinese say, very gently.

# Age

*Growing old is a bad habit which a busy man has no time to form.*

ANDRÉ MAUROIS

The Romans of classical antiquity valued old age, and honoured it with the principle of *seniores priores*, in which the respect due to experience gave it a front seat at the counsels of state. Even if it is true, as La Rochefoucauld observed, that 'old men like to give good advice to console themselves for no longer being able to set bad examples', it is nevertheless useful to a society to have the fruits of experience available if required. The Chinese take this to an extreme; in their gerontocracy no one under seventy-five is regarded as yet fit for power. They think time induces perspective – as exemplified by Zhou En Lai's celebrated comment on the French Revolution: when asked whether he thought it had been a good thing, he said (after a pause for deliberation), 'It's too soon to say.'

The fashion in recent times has been for the young to hold centre stage, as if they were the only important form of human being. The main reason is that advertisers know that the young have beliefs they are prepared to back with money, chief among them that everyone else is having fun, and that if they are to have fun too they must go somewhere smoky and noisy and wear the same clothes as the others there. They therefore flock to clubs or Ibiza in search of stupefaction by a combination of decibels, drink and drugs, and mock their elders for flinching from the scene. They do not see that 'nobody loves life like an old man', as Sophocles remarked, and that accumulated years confer wisdom of the kind possessed by the old bull in the fable (which goes: a young bull sees that the gate into the next field, full of cows, is open. In delight he says to the old bull, 'Look! The gate's open! Let's rush down there and have a few!' To which the old bull replies, 'No; let's go down there slowly, and have them all').

There is, incidentally, no such thing as 'middle age'. This is the period of life when, allegedly, your broad mind and narrow waist change places, or when, as Franklin Adams observed, you are too young to take up bowls but too old to rush up to the net at tennis. Some people are born old, and some die young in their nineties: it is entirely a matter of attitude, which, as the Stoics long ago pointed out, is something at your own command. What happens as the years pass is that folly somewhat abates, and the bank balance improves; on both counts, getting older is a desirable activity.

There is much false propaganda about age. 'Age has a good mind and sorry shanks,' said Aretino, confusing the ability to run for a bus with good health. Most of the saws and sayings that apply to age, making it a concoction of trembling limbs and forgetfulness, are drawn from a time when people were old at forty. A person must now be at least double that to have the honour of being properly old. And honour it is: 'Life is a country that the old have seen, and lived in,' said Joseph Joubert; 'those who have yet to travel through it can only learn the way from them.'

# Gifts

*Even a little gift may be vast with loving-kindness.*

THEOCRITUS

Almost everyone agrees that the value of a gift cannot be measured by its price. No sum can quantify the worth of a gift which is appropriate, timely, thoughtful, well-chosen, or given with real friendship or love. Such gifts convey part of the giver's self; they represent the portion of his history devoted to thinking about the recipient, and to seeking and choosing for him something that will speak his sentiments.

Even the merest gifts of duty, handed out at conventional times of year, oblige givers to think about recipients in a particular way – namely, in respect of their character, interests and needs, because these are what constrain the choice of present. Lavender-scented bath salts are somewhat misplaced for most muddy-kneed boys, as a plastic cap-firing gun might be for most elderly aunts. At least to the extent of recognising structural factors about another person's biography and its unfolding, the duty to give a present is a salutary one. But duty-given gifts are otherwise worthless, because they carry no heart in them.

The best gifts do not come in wrapping-paper. They take the form of attitudes, of gestures and sentiments, of solidarity and pertinent aid in its season. Consider the tradition established by Rikkyu-No-Sen, Japan's greatest tea master, in which a host who has invited a friend to tea decorates his room with a spray of blossom and an inscription chosen to celebrate their friendship. In the refinement of the choice lies the tenderness of the act, and with it the largeness of the gift it represents.

But gifts are complicated things. 'An enemy's gift is ruinous and no gift,' said Sophocles. Anything given in expectation of return, or expressly creating an obligation, can prove too costly for the recipient, though free at the time of receipt. 'Gifts are hooks,' cautioned Martial. An allied consideration is that a recipient can come to feel resentment towards the donor, whether or not his belief that the gift concealed a hook is true. Givers feel better-disposed towards receivers than vice versa; it is charming and warming to give, for not much can adulterate the self-satisfaction involved – except of course ill-graced ingratitude or even mere indifference on the receiver's part. But the receiver has to express pleasure and thanks that might not be felt in the quantity standardly required, and is anyway thereafter at the disadvantage of being a debtor. 'We do not quite forgive a giver,' Emerson remarked. 'The hand that feeds us is in some danger of being bitten.'

There is a saying, 'Bis dat qui cito dat,' meaning 'He gives twice who gives quickly'. Dr Johnson, whose famous line 'Slow rises worth by poverty depressed' was squeezed out of him by bitter experience, sought patronage from the Earl of Bute, and was offered it only when he had at last become famous. In his letter of disdainful refusal he wrote, 'Let him that desires to see others happy make haste to give ... every moment of delay takes away something from the value of his benefaction.'

Dr Johnson's resentment reminds one of a further complication: that some people are very hard to give presents to. Suspicious and prickly recipients will always find a complaint to make, whatever one gives; sometimes the intended recipient is so much one's peer, or so idiosyncratic in his tastes, that selecting a genuinely appropriate gift seems impossible.

Emerson – a disliker of the whole system of giving and getting – added, 'How painful to give a gift to any person of sensibility, or of equality! It is next worst to receiving one.'

The easiest people to please with a gift are those whose wide interests and generous enthusiasms make them spring to mind in every shop. But such folk are surprisingly rare. For most choosers of gifts the deepest dilemma of giving remains. 'I know what I have given you,' Antonio Porchia wrote, 'but I do not know what you have received.' A sobering thought; but it reveals this related truth too: if you know what the recipient has received on receiving your gift, either you know him well, or love him much – or both.

# Trifles

According to received wisdom, the holiday month of August deserves its sobriquet of 'the Silly Season' because absence of major news – by which is meant political stories, most party leaders being on holiday – obliges news organisations to grope for matter to fill their bulletins. What they find is invariably regarded as trivial. Typical offerings include a story about a human head found inside a giant cod and a London man's achieving a world-record eructation of 118 decibels. Both these examples are culled from a single August's offerings, and could be supplemented by dozens more.

A student of the news media might point out that this fare is the staple of tabloid newspapers all year round, and only becomes comment-worthy when broadsheets and broadcasters resort to its like in the dog days of summer. But dismissing such stories as trifles misses a point. Trifles are the texture of history; in minutiae lie truths, and more significance attaches to the myriad of events unobvious or apparently mundane than to single grand upheavals. As Manuel Gonzalez Prada said, 'The displacement of a little sand eventually changes the deepest river's course.'

There are at least two senses in which something can count

as a trifle: one, by being small or unobvious, and the other, by being ordinary, familiar or mundane. In both cases it takes observation to single it out and see it for what it is. 'It is only the dullness of the eye' – to quote Walter Pater – 'that makes any two things seem alike.' The small might be lost to view in the world's sheer multiplicity, and the mundane likewise because ordinariness always confers invisibility. To be able to see such things in their own right is a special talent, but it is one that can be acquired by mindfulness and attention. The ability to see the small and the ordinary in their full particularity brings the texture of the world richly into view, and surprises one because it shows that small things can be large in meaning, and that scarcely anything is ordinary after all.

Pliny the Younger remarked that people travel far to see things which, if they were under their noses, would lie neglected and unconsidered. That suggests one should inhabit one's life like a traveller, curious and alert, looking for the strangeness in things in order to seem them afresh. To survive the blunting effects of time and habit on our sensibilities, we do well to remember the rousing claims of Carlyle, who said that the meanest object is a window into infinitude, and Rilke, in his remarkable *Letters to a Young Poet*, who said that if the world does not appear magical, 'blame yourself; tell yourself that you are not poet enough to call forth its riches.'

There are less exalted reasons for giving little things their due. They can give peace, and consolation, just as they can give distress out of proportion to their scale. The greater part of most ordinary biographies is a record of what was individually set in a minor key, and there is not much space between those apparent trifles that engender dissatisfaction and a sense of defeat, and those that yield recurring pleasure, giving the quality of life a positive cast. To say that trifles make up the happiness or the misery of human life is to voice a cliché no less true for being one, and no less worth remembering.

If one sees the importance of small things, one is better able to judge the importance of their opposite. If only for this reason it is well that trifles are interesting, because they exercise our sense of perspective, and help us calibrate the material of experience. 'For the person for whom small things do not exist,' said Ortega y Gasset, 'the great is not great.' Such a person has no sense of proportion, which is a terrible defect because the ability to measure things is essential to judgment and – as a consequence – to the task of living well.